THE
HOT SAUCE
PRINCIPLE

How To Live And Lead In A World Where Everything Is Urgent All Of The Time

— BRANDON M. SMITH —

INDIE BOOKS
INTERNATIONAL

ISBN: 978-1-952233-09-8
Library of Congress Control Number: 2020906437

Designed by Joni McPherson, mcphersongraphics.com

INDIE BOOKS INTERNATIONAL, INC
2424 VISTA WAY, SUITE 316
OCEANSIDE, CA 92054
www.indiebooksintl.com

— CONTENTS —

Preface..v

PART ONE • THE URGENCY EPIDEMIC 1

Chapter 1   Monday Morning.........................3

Chapter 2   The Urgency Epidemic 11

Chapter 3   The Good, The Bad, And The Ugly Of A Hot
Sauce World 25

PART TWO • LEADING WITH URGENCY...........43

Chapter 4   Preparing Your Kitchen...................45

Chapter 5   Cooking With Hot Sauce 65

Chapter 6   The Dangers Of Cooking With Hot Sauce 85

**PART THREE • PROTECTING YOURSELF FROM
GETTING BURNED**................................99

Chapter 7   Protecting Yourself And Your Team From
The Heat..............................101

Chapter 8   Cooking With Hot Sauce At Home.........121

Chapter 9   Mastering Urgency......................143

APPENDIX

Acknowledgments 149

About The Author.............................151

— INTRODUCTION —
The Purpose of This Book

We are in the middle of an urgency epidemic. These are the words I used to begin Chapter 2 of this book as I wrote in the late months of 2018. Little did I know that a little more than a year later an actual global pandemic would overtake our lives and forever alter the ways in which we conduct our daily business. I was preparing the final book details and prepping for launch with my editor when the world seemed to shut down in March 2020. I felt a momentary sense of panic: had the book I spent all these months writing suddenly become obsolete? Grounded by COVID-19, many of us no longer had to dash out the door predawn to beat traffic for a meeting-filled day at the office. Nor did we have the pressure to rush home to shuffle kids to various practices, rehearsals or tutoring sessions. Had the Urgency Epidemic inadvertently been cured overnight?

And then my phone began ringing and my email began to pile up with messages from people who were overwhelmed in a new way. Their work hadn't simply disappeared: now they were being asked to do their work while juggling kids on the home front. They needed to learn new technology now and implement it into their daily routines today. In addition, the urgency for those working on the "front lines" was at an all-time high. Almost as quickly as my fear of obsoletion had developed, it disappeared.

As someone who has studied workplace functionality in a myriad of industries and coached hundreds of mid and executive corporate leaders for nearly two decades, I've had a front-row spectator's seat to the evolution of the urgency epidemic. I have heard it from my clients, former students and workplace "warriors;" they are overwhelmed and at a loss as to how to proceed in an environment that cuts them no slack, provides no respite, and is ever pushing them on. When I speak to groups, I often describe the sensation as one where it feels like hot sauce is on everything. What do I mean by that? In the world of cooking, great chefs use hot sauce with skill only to enhance the naturally underlying flavors of their meals; the purpose of hot sauce is not supposed to be to purposefully cause esophageal damage to a patron, it's supposed to make the meal better, to add to the experience by bringing to the forefront the flavor details the chef wants you to pay most attention to.

But imagine, for a moment, going into a restaurant and sitting down to place your order. You peruse the menu, and after careful consideration, order a soup, a salad and entrée. You even decide to splurge on their famous dessert. One by one, the waiter delivers each course. But, to your shock, everything is covered in hot sauce. And not in a good way. Your salad is dripping with it. Your soup seems to be straight out of the hot sauce bottle. Your entrée and the sides are swimming in it, and even the delicious dessert is drowning in the stuff. By this point, it doesn't matter. You couldn't appreciate the dessert, even if you wanted to. Your mouth is on fire, your eyes are watering, you are dripping with sweat and you can't actually taste a thing. Slowly, your taste buds are becoming numb to all of it, and all flavor, except "hot" is lost.

This is what it feels like to have uncontrolled urgency in our lives. Everything is covered in hot sauce, and often we lose the ability to distinguish differences between what is being "served" our way. In other words, everything feels like it brings a sense of urgency, from what we hear from our bosses, our direct reports, our clients, and even our loved ones at home. Our body revolts and we want relief as we stand precariously on the brink of burn-out, only to see another course drenched in hot sauce coming our way.

It isn't too late; you don't have to send it all back to the kitchen. The purpose of this book is to guide you through the urgency epidemic and put you back in charge. Specifically, the following areas will be addressed:

If you are a leader, learn how to properly use urgency to motivate rather than burn out your team. How can you effectively put hot sauce on the right things (and not on everything leaving your kitchen)?

If you are the recipient of others' urgency, how can you properly respond so as to not allow others to infect you? How can you protect yourself and keep yourself balanced? In other words, what do you do when you're served a dessert swimming in hot sauce?

How to keep yourself and your family safe from the urgency epidemic? When should you use urgency at home and when should you not? What's the appropriate amount of hot sauce to use with your spouse? Your kids? With your volunteer position?

This book is designed to help you become a master of urgency. Like a great chef, you'll learn the nuances of adding just the right amount of sauce to bring out the deep flavor and potential of yourself, your team, and your family, creating a menu of balance and perfect spice so that you are in charge of urgency and it no longer consumes your world. Let's begin.

Brandon Smith
May 2020

— PART ONE —

THE URGENCY EPIDEMIC

— CHAPTER 1 —
Monday Morning

 Kate's hands shook as she pressed them against the marble countertop. She stared at them closely, wondering if she could will them to stop.

She didn't have time for this. Kate looked up and saw her furrowed brow in the bathroom mirror. It was 5:30 a.m. on Monday. This was not how Kate had wanted her week to begin. She slowly closed her eyes and took a deep breath. Unfortunately, this was not an uncommon start to her days, particularly Mondays.

Kate released her deep breath and tried to logically assess the situation. "Okay, Kate," she said to herself, "on a scale of one to ten, what level would you score the anxiety you're feeling?" She was channeling her therapist, Eileen, as she mouthed the words. The answer immediately popped into her mind: 8.5.

Not the score she wanted today, of all days. Kate opened her eyes. She wasn't sure how she was going to get it all done. Her mind quickly inventoried all the to-do's and demands that were facing her this week.

There was Martin. Kate had worked for Martin for the last year, and it had been one of the more difficult years of her professional life. What made it particularly complicated was that Kate liked Martin. He wasn't a bad guy. Martin had three kids just a few years older than Kate's and he regularly joked with her about the challenges of parenting teenagers. He would regularly open meetings with a funny *dad joke* or a story about one of his kids.

Martin really was a good guy, but as a boss, if Kate was gut-level honest, he made her life miserable. Kate oversaw a new technology upgrade across the company and Martin was the Chief Technology Officer. From a technology standpoint, Kate's company was behind. It not only lagged their competitors' offerings, but there was also a pressing need to upgrade how customer data was protected. The Board was pushing hard on senior leadership to make these changes yesterday. And while Martin meant well, he pushed all that pressure and urgency down to Kate and her team.

Kate paused from brushing her hair to look down at her phone. It was now 5:35 a.m. and her phone flashed with a new email from Martin. The subject line was: "Emergency meeting today at 8 a.m. to discuss status of technology upgrades." Kate grabbed her phone angrily and flipped it over so she couldn't see the screen. She hoped that if she couldn't see it, she wouldn't feel the pressure. "Out of sight, out of mind," she sighed.

Martin's email sent Kate's mind to the events of the prior week when Martin had called another one of these last-minute, "emergency" meetings to discuss the status of her team's projects. It had been Sunday afternoon when Kate received his meeting email. She and her team were still in the office trying to get ahead for the week, when Kate had looked down at her phone and saw Martin's meeting invite. She'd sighed and in exhaustion, flipped her phone over.

Almost simultaneously, there had been a light knock at her door. She had looked up as Amanda, her most trusted direct report and most competent team member, entered her office. "Kate, can I talk to you for a minute?" she had asked.

Immediately, Kate had felt her stomach begin to clench. Sure enough, Amanda had proceeded to tell her that she could no longer take the pace that they had been running at for the past nine months. Amanda had two children under the age of three and was hardly seeing them on the weekends let alone during the week. Her husband was doing the best he could to juggle his own work commitments and the kids, but after a very long conversation the night before, Amanda and her husband had come to the decision that something had to give.

As Amanda finished her explanation, she handed over her two-week notice to Kate. To be honest, Kate had only really heard half of Amanda's explanation as her thoughts raced ahead. How was she going to get everything done without Amanda? The team was already behind. Kate also knew that asking for more help was a non-starter. The entire organization had instituted a hiring freeze across the board, even including open positions that were the result of critical employees leaving the company for better opportunities. Just getting Amanda's role backfilled was going to be a fight.

The next day, Kate had met with Martin at 8 a.m. to review the status of her team's work. "Kate, I just met with the senior leadership team," Martin began. "We are experiencing tremendous pressure from our investors to get our technology platforms up and running this quarter."

Kate had sat back and listened quietly, hoping that if she was quiet enough, Martin wouldn't add any more to her plate. That strategy never seemed to work. Martin paused and appeared to look out the window for a moment, and then returned his gaze to Kate.

Martin continued: "I want your team to not only accelerate your timeline with this initiative, but I also want the customer data protocols set up at the same time. In addition, I need your group to investigate how you can be gathering more data on our customers for the sales team. This is a new request that has come up from the Board. They believe that we need to be doing more to gather customer data and, in addition to protecting it, we need to be conducting more sophisticated analysis to anticipate market trends and customer needs. I need your team on that right away."

Martin paused and looked at Kate. Kate looked back and flatly said, "Amanda just gave her two-week notice."

Kate gauged Martin's face to see if he got the magnitude of her statement.

Without missing a beat, he responded, "That is a real loss. Amanda is a strong team player. Any chance we could keep her?" After Kate explained that Amanda had made up her mind and that the pace and volume of work was the reason, Martin began to appear defensive.

"Martin, I need to not only replace Amanda's position ASAP, but I need approval to hire two more people," Kate offered.

After appearing to consider Kate's request, Martin shook his head and replied, "I'm sorry Kate. My hands are really tied. You are going to have to do the best you can with what you have."

"Do the best you can with what you have." Martin's words echoed in Kate's mind as she moved from brushing her hair to giving her face a more serious examination. Her eyes did look tired. As much as she wanted to blame the poor bathroom lighting, she had to reluctantly admit it. Kate peered more closely and could see the bags under eyes.

"Mom, you need to get more rest," Kate's 14 year-old daughter Ainsley had commented just days ago. Kate was exhausted and she wasn't too proud to deny it. She also knew that when she got tired, her first mental move was to beat herself up for her failures as a parent, real or imagined. That soundtrack of nagging worry was a familiar one: She hasn't been involved enough. She hasn't been preparing her kids enough. She hasn't been present enough. The barrage of school e-mails she received on any given day only made it worse. Emails such as:

> *Hi Parents. This is your child's ninth grade math teacher. We move fast in my classroom to prepare your child with the opportunity to take post-calculus, college-level mathematics for engineers by their junior or senior year. If your child is in my classroom, it is safe to assume that they are probably already behind. Our goal is to get them caught up with the goal of equipping them to get into the dream school of their choice...*

> *Hi Parents. This is your seven-year-old child's baseball coach. I'm excited to be coaching your child this season. Our goal is to grow your child's skills so he can not only grow his love for the game, but also so he can become a highly skilled player. It is important to know that I coach my teams to win. In order to accomplish that goal, I will need your full participation. We practice a minimum of*

three times a week in addition to games twice a week. While this schedule is more than most coaches in our league, I have found that it pays off in the long run. Many of my former players have gone on to play travel baseball and ultimately get college scholarships. I am committed to helping your seven-year-old get there too...

Kate wanted to say that none of it really mattered, but all her friends seemed to be caught up in the same race. When she got the rare opportunity to go to one of her book club gatherings, the conversation inevitably turned to all the things that the rest of the moms were doing to get their kids a leg up in applying for college. Never mind that most of their kids haven't completed elementary school yet.

Kate fished out her concealer from her drawer and began to work on the bags under eyes. She might be able to admit to herself that she's tired, but she definitely didn't want anyone else to notice.

Her phone began to vibrate. Kate rolled her eyes. It was probably Martin again. The week ahead looked about as bleak as any of the weeks she had endured in recent memory. Full days of meetings, late nights and an increasing pile of "urgent" items that she and her team would never be able to get to.

Kate's hands began to shake again. She put down her concealer brush and let her eyes drift back to her hands. She felt perpetually behind with not enough time in the day or week to meet everyone's expectations and demands. No matter how hard she tried, it never seemed good enough. Kate reached for the bottle of anxiety medication that Dr. Sheth had prescribed her, realizing even that didn't seem to be helping any more.

She popped the pills in her mouth and washed them down with water from the cup next to her sink as her hands continued to shake.

— CHAPTER 2 —
The Urgency Epidemic

 It was still dark at 6:30 a.m. Kate put her coffee in her cup holder and slowly eased out of her driveway. She had planned to take her kids to school that morning, but Martin's "emergency meeting" forced her to change her plans. As she made the left turn out of her cul-de-sac, she turned on her radio to find something that would distract her from the noise in her head and the overwhelming anxiety she felt.

This part of her commute was the best. She made the right at the first stop sign and then a left at the next. There was a stillness and quiet at that time of the morning in her neighborhood that she just loved.

As she approached the entrance of her neighborhood, reality hit. At the intersection ahead, Kate saw the countless car lights piercing the calm darkness of the morning. There were rows of cars three lanes deep barely moving. Kate needed to merge into that crowd and somehow get to her office in time for Martin's meeting. "This is easily going to be an hour-and-a-half commute," Kate thought to herself.

Her hands tensed around the steering wheel as she eased closer to her turn to merge into the crowd. Once it became Kate's turn to merge into the crowd, one by one, drivers ignored her as they continued to inch their cars forward. Every driver looked the same to Kate. They were gripping their steering wheels, staring straight ahead with anxious and desperate looks in their eyes. They obviously knew Kate was trying to merge, and yet they seemed to intentionally avoid eye contact with her so they wouldn't feel obligated to let her in. "Looks like everyone has an emergency meeting to get to," Kate thought to herself.

It wasn't always like this. When Kate and her husband moved into their house back in 2005, life felt different. And not just because they didn't have the chaos that comes with three kids. Work felt different. Rush hour was a predictable window, and rarely was there bumper-to-bumper traffic at 6:30 a.m. or before 4:30 p.m.

In addition, there wasn't a smartphone sitting in the car cup holder, pinging at every minute of the commute, or every minute of the day, for that matter. But, most importantly, it seemed like the work demands were *manageable*. Was that really the case or was she just feeling nostalgic, Kate wondered to herself.

Kate recalled her first technology transformation project. The timeline was something like eighteen months, unlike the insane six-month timelines she and her team get today. She recalled that during that entire project, the team she was on didn't lose one team member. Not one. In addition, if the team needed resources, all they had to do was make a strong case, and the resources appeared. That wasn't to say there weren't long days or serious pushes as her team approached *go-live* dates. There definitely were. But those were predictable and planned sprints. Today, it felt like she was being told to sprint until she and her team dropped. There is no time for rest and there is no predictability to the intensity. Everything felt urgent, and there was a need to be on the alert at every moment.

At that moment, an opening appeared in traffic. Kate quickly hit the gas and found her place in the mass of cars making their way down the highway. As she looked in her rearview mirror to thank the driver behind her, she realized that they had not even noticed her trying to merge into traffic. All Kate could see was the top of the driver's head as they looked down at their phone. As traffic backed up behind them, a series of honks jerked that driver's head upward and their car took an uncomfortable lurch forward. "Times have definitely changed," Kate thought to herself as she settled into her long commute. "Now, if only I am lucky enough to make it in time for the start of the meeting," she thought.

The Urgency Epidemic

We are in the middle of an urgency epidemic. I'm sure this comes as no major revelation to you, dear reader. You are reading this book. What may come as a surprise to you is that you are not alone. Everyone I meet, regardless of what they do or where they live in the world is experiencing this overwhelming sense of urgency. We can sum this up in two simple statements:

Time is everyone's most precious resource.

and

It feels like everything is urgent all the time.

I would wager that you are nodding your head in agreement with those simple, yet profound statements. "Yep, I don't have enough time to get stuff done, and yep, everything feels like it has to be done right now." I'm as guilty as the next person to succumbing to this infection. I can't tell you how many times in each day I respond to a fresh email with urgency, when, in fact, that email could probably wait days, if not longer, for a response. Consider the following low-urgency emails that I might receive on any given day:

Brandon, we are looking forward to having you at our retreat next month. Do you have any dietary requirements or lunch requests?

Brandon, I am thrilled that you invited me to come on your podcast. I look forward to hearing from you and your producers so we can schedule a date for the show over the next few months.

Dear Professor Smith, I was a student of yours several years ago. I have run into a career challenge. Would you have time for a brief call? I look forward to reconnecting.

I'm sure you get similar types of emails. People wanting to meet for coffee. Others asking if you will be able to attend a social outing. All the above emails are varying degrees of important, but none would we classify as urgent. And yet, I treat them as if they are urgent *and* important. I know better, but I can't help myself.

But it wasn't always like this. There was a time, in the not-so-distant past, when work existed primarily at the place where one would go to do work.

When the workday was done, one hopped in their car and left their work at work. When they got home, there was time to connect and reconnect with their family. There were still math tutors and baseball practice, but the pace and urgency of even those activities was different. If your boss needed you, you were called on your home phone. Hence, bosses rarely called people at home. Results were expected over a year, not quarter by quarter. We knew our coworkers as people because we would regularly go to lunch with them. We would typically work for the same employer for years, sometimes decades. We felt urgency, but it wasn't a daily co-pilot with us. When we had to act with urgency, we did, knowing that a state of rest and preparation typically would follow.

Does the picture seem absurd? For some people, this picture was as recent as the year 2000. For all of us, this picture was *normal* before the mid-1990s. So, what happened?

The Rise Of The Urgency Epidemic: How Did We Get Here?

Unlike most epidemics, urgency doesn't have its roots in a *patient zero*. Many factors have brought us to this point. Consider the following:

Portable Technology. In the not-so-distant past, there existed a requirement that to do office work, we needed to be *in the office*. While smartphones have been a technological and communication breakthrough, they have had an unintended consequence on our lives. The smartphone broke any natural boundaries that existed between our work lives and our personal lives. Now, we can receive work-related communications any time and any place. And with that ability to receive that information, it has created the expectation that, therefore, we should be available 24/7. We have more information coming to us at all hours of the day. Ironically, rather than streamline communication, smartphone technology has made the world noisier. Our choice becomes simple: ignore the information coming our way and deal with the hundreds of *urgent* requests on Monday morning or take them on as they come, regardless of the day or time. It doesn't seem like much of a choice at all.

Rapid Technology Changes Inside Organizations. Beyond our personal use of technology, there is a consistently rapid increase in the demand for technology upgrades in our workplace. How can we further automate how we do things? We must keep up with industry trends. We must find ways to do things smarter, faster, and leaner.

Show me a workplace, and I promise you that something related to a technology-related initiative is causing them to lose sleep.

I was speaking to a senior leader of a Fortune 500 company recently and he so simply and eloquently described this trend in this way as he spoke about his company: "Historically, we have always been a great service company that also offered technology solutions. Now, we have to transform ourselves into a technology company with great service." No easy task, particularly given the insanely aggressive timelines that most companies are operating under to achieve such a monumental transformation.

Pervasive Industry Changes And Destabilization. Examining the last fifty years of modern workplaces, one would be hard-pressed to find a time with as much industry destabilization as there is today. Even before the concerns that COVID-19 presented, brick-and-mortar retailers were questioning how many stores to close as greater customer demand has moved to online. Traditional media continues to transform from newsstands and networks to something else. Healthcare costs continue to rise with no clear solution in sight. Higher education costs have increased, questioning the future of in-classroom learning. Younger generations want to interact with businesses and organizations differently. Big companies are all struggling to adapt to the changes thrust upon them. Change is everywhere. The urgency to adapt is greater than ever.

Recessions, Depressions & Pandemics Leave Battle Scars. When the global recession hit in 2008-2009, organizations were rocked resulting in mass layoffs and mantras of "do more with less." As a result, most organizations made the conscious or unconscious choice to remain lean and not rehire or fill open positions. A former student shared this story with me several years ago:

> *I was working for this company going into 2008. I had a team of three people supporting the work we were doing, and we were functioning very strategically. Then the recession hit. All my team was eliminated, but I remained. My boss gave me clear instructions to continue to keep everything moving forward all by myself. I worked harder than ever the next few years. I had to shift from strategic work to day-to-day tactical work because I didn't have anyone to help me with that. When the results came in, everyone's expectations were exceeded. My boss gave me a huge "Congratulations!" Our profits were back and even ahead of where we were pre-recession. Thrilled, I took that as an opportunity to ask for permission to start rebuilding my team. My boss looked me squarely in the eye and with a smile said, "Absolutely not! Why would we do that? You are doing a great job. Keep it up." It was then that I realized I wasn't running a marathon. I was running until I dropped.*

Since 2008, the mantra of "do more with less" has been pervasive. Lean benches are an understatement. Using a baseball analogy, it is as if we are playing not only without any bench players, there isn't anyone playing second base or center field. As a result, there are no *routine plays*. Everything is urgent and fires are imminent.

Unrealistic Pressure From The Marketplace, Shareholders, And Stakeholders. With all the factors above, investors and other influencers are pressing on leadership to make changes at lightning speed. Rather than pushing back, most leaders push that pressure down into their organization in the same way they hear and feel it. In other words, the message gets sent throughout the organization that "We aren't moving fast enough. We need to accelerate our change. We need to change everything right now. Go!"

The result of the factors above is an epidemic of global proportions. No one is immune and there is no place to hide. More importantly, the costs will be great if we don't right the ship.

What Does A World Smothered In Urgency Hot Sauce Look Like?

Imagine looking a decade into the future with my magic crystal ball, but the ball only shows the bad. Assume that the urgency epidemic has spread like wildfire and no one has learned to master this growing cancer. Imagine what destruction you might see. Consider all these possible long-term costs to our society if we don't learn how to master this threat.

Our Attention Span Approaches Zero. A world with everything urgent is a world without focus. We move from one pressing demand to another. We become distracted easily and perpetually multitask. A simple example of this is how our attention span has shifted dramatically in how we consume content online. Several years ago, I had the opportunity to give a TED talk. When preparing for the talk, the organizers shared this with me: "While a TED talk can be twenty or so minutes, we find viewership drops off after fifteen minutes." I proceeded to deliver my talk in 14:59, and promptly patted myself on the back for hitting the threshold. To my disappointment, the next year I learned the TED organizers were advising TED talk speakers that viewership was now dropping off after nine minutes. To offer another example, I was recently speaking to a senior communications officer for a fast food restaurant company about how she goes about getting her organization's attention when everything is urgent all the time. Her comment to me was even more striking. When putting out videos to the organization related to mission-critical initiatives, the videos must be three minutes or less. If they aren't, the videos wouldn't be watched at all. People just can't sit still that long. It is as if the entire human population is being diagnosed with Attention Deficit Hyperactivity Disorder (ADHD). If this continues, just imagine all the lost car keys.

We Can't Distinguish Between What Is Important And What Isn't. Steven Covey developed his famous "Urgent vs. Important" 2 x 2 matrix many years ago. The principle is simple. Identify the things that are both urgent and important and do those things first. Next identify the things that are important but not urgent and do those things second. Then, do the things that might be urgent but not important. Finally, don't do the things that are neither urgent nor important. Makes sense. However, in a world where we're being told everything is urgent, it is virtually impossible to distinguish between what is important from what isn't. As the hot sauce is poured over everything in our lives, it all tastes the same. Hence, we evaluate it all as "important." I bet you've succumbed to this trap some time over the last forty-eight hours. Let's test my hypothesis. I would wager that someone sent you a message that was urgent, but not important. And, rather than saying to yourself, "this can wait," you quickly responded. If we can't identify what is truly important, and nurture those things, we run the risk of our lives being consumed by unimportant "urgent" activities.

We All Become Firefighters. With the hot sauce on every-thing, an inability to focus and an inability to assess what is important, we will all become (and are becoming) firefighters. "Why is this bad?" you might ask. Simple.

With everyone focused on and actively fighting fires, no one will be thinking about how to prevent them.

Ironically, our inability to proactively prevent fires will increase the number of fires (or problems) in our lives. Have you ever had a situation in which you knew you needed to address something, but you put it off because you didn't have time? As a result, the issue went from a small ember to a raging multi-acre forest fire. I can give you a personal example. I noticed that when I was driving my car and coming to a stop, the brakes were squeaking. At first, it was a subtle squeak. I told myself, "I bet that is someone else's car that I'm hearing." Then the noise became more pronounced. My self-talk rationalization moved to this beauty, "I bet the brakes are squeaking because of the weather" (it just rained, it hasn't rained for days, etc.). Soon, I surrendered to the reality that yes, my brakes did not sound good. I made an appointment with the dealership and took my car in. Yes, indeed, the brakes needed to be replaced. Unfortunately, by the time I took the car in, it was one week past the expiration of my warranty. Total bill = $2,000.00 (yes, I know, I probably paid too much). A firefighter mindset, ironically, just promotes bigger fires. Rather than dealing with something when it is a squeak, we wait until the squeak becomes costly.

We Suffer Burnout and Loss. This picture of a world consumed by urgency is an unsustainable one. Ultimately, this extreme world will lead to pervasive burnout. We will walk away from jobs, relationships and other commitments in our lives because we just can't do it anymore. We'll have had enough. As I write this book, there is a growing phenomenon with younger workers in their late twenties and thirties walking away from high-paying jobs and promising careers, not to mention the growing statistics of anxiety, depression, and addiction previously mentioned.

Clearly, this is not a happy picture or one many of us would want to come to fruition. We must do what we can to prevent it. Throughout the chapters in this book, we will treat and cure this illness. But, with any problem, issue or illness, the first step is a "diagnosis." Review the questions at the end of this chapter to determine the degree to which you are suffering from this urgency epidemic.

CHAPTER 2 QUESTIONS TO CONSIDER

1. In what ways does your phone and other technology contribute to the urgency you experience?

2. How able do you feel you are to "turn off" the technology urgency you feel when you need to? Rate yourself on the scale below:

PROACTIVE	REACTIVE
I am a master of the technology hot sauce, limiting it at specific times of the day and week.	I am a slave to my phone and/or laptop. My phone sleeps under my pillow every night.

3. What industry/market pressures have you experienced that have increased the daily urgency you feel?

4. Have you noticed that your attention and ability to focus has changed in recent years? If so, how?

5. In what ways can you relate to feeling like a "firefighter"?

6. When was the last time you felt burned-out?

7. What role did urgency play in your feeling that way?

CHAPTER 3
The Good, The Bad, And The Ugly Of Urgency

 8:11 a.m. Kate was approaching the meeting room that Martin had secured for their discussion. Peering in through the glass, Kate could see that Martin had already started the meeting. Most of her team was present, and judging by their body language, no one appeared very excited to be there. Martin, on the other hand, seemed to be animated. His hands were in constant motion and he began to point to a few items on the whiteboard. Kate took a deep breath and entered the room.

"…if we don't accelerate this timeline, we won't have the necessary progress that the senior leadership team needs to see at the end of next quarter…" Martin trailed off with Kate's arrival. Trying not to appear irritated with Kate's late entrance, acting as though he was pleasantly surprised, Martin smoothly said, "Kate, I was just informing the team about the newly updated timelines and the importance of our accelerated pace."

Kate didn't say a word. She sat down and pulled out her laptop to look like she was prepared and ready to go. Over the next fifteen minutes, the meeting proceeded in Martin's typical fashion. Martin would lecture the group stressing the importance and urgency of the situation while the group stared blankly back at Martin. Eventually, Martin moved the meeting toward conclusion, "Now that we are all aligned around this new timeline, I look forward to your status updates. If you need anything from me, don't hesitate to ask." There was a quick shuffling of laptops in bags, and soon, everyone had cleared out of the room. Everyone except Kate.

Martin was busily cleaning up the whiteboard, unaware that Kate had not left the room. Kate broke the silence. "Martin, can I speak with you for a moment?"

Startled, Martin replied, "Oh, hey, Kate. Of course. I didn't know you were still hanging around." Kate was about to speak when Martin continued, "I thought that was a very productive meeting, don't you think?"

Kate paused for a moment as she processed the many ways she could respond to Martin's observation. She took another deep breath, mustered her courage, and replied, "No, Martin. I don't think that meeting went well at all. Did you see my team? They didn't respond to any of your questions or new direction. Not even once. That silence wasn't acceptance that you received. That was apathy. They are becoming desensitized to the repeated drum beat of 'we are behind, and we must go faster.' All they are hearing is that no matter what they do, it will never be good enough, and any hopes of getting a break from this crazy pace is out the door. Not to mention, we have been begging for additional resources for months, and we constantly get told no. At some point, something has to give."

Kate paused for a response, holding her breath as she wondered how Martin was going to react. Martin's face moved from stunned to irritated to calm in a matter of seconds. He pulled back a chair and sat down at the conference room table.

"Kate, I hear you. Yes, we have not been able to get the resources that you have been requesting, and yes, we have been getting more and more aggressive with our timelines. And, while I know this has been hard on your team, I believe in you and your team." Martin paused to let his last comment sink in with Kate. "Do you remember the payroll system upgrade that we completed four years ago?" Martin asked.

"Of course, I do," Kate replied. "That was one of the most disorganized, frustrating and messy projects that my team and I ever worked on."

"And what happened?" Martin asked.

Kate didn't have to think long about that painful project. She quickly responded, "Well, for one, our timeline kept getting moved up. At one point I think the entire timeline had been cut in half from the one originally proposed. In addition, many of our key partners in HR left the company, so we were flying blind. We didn't have any knowledge of what HR needed and how they used the information that we were creating for them. And, on top of it all, we had to pull multiple all-nighters when we turned on the system due to so many technical issues."

A small smile crept across Martin's face. "And then what happened?"

At that moment, Kate saw where Martin was taking this conversation. Reluctantly, she continued, "We hit the deadline, for one. In addition, there were no issues and complaints once we worked through the kinks the days prior to the deadline, something that had never happened with these types of system overhauls. It moved us lightyears into the future from an HR technology standpoint. It was one of the biggest 'impossible' accomplishments that my team had ever achieved."

Martin looked at Kate, and with a Cheshire cat grin said, "And it got you promoted."

As Kate left the meeting room and made her way to her desk, her mind was spinning. On the one hand, the demands, pressure, and urgency on her team seemed ridiculous. Her team could only take so much, and she felt confident that they had already crossed that point. On the other hand, Martin made a compelling point. She and her team had been here before, and they pulled it off then. Maybe she wasn't pushing her team enough. Maybe they were capable of more than she was giving them credit for. Was this intense pressure going to break her team or was it just what they needed?

Is Urgency Good Or Bad?

Back in the early 1930s, the Southeastern part of the United States was hit with both the Great Depression and one of the worst droughts in recorded history. A soil conservation commission was formed, and they soon began championing a lesser-known Japanese vine called kudzu to replace drought ravaged native ground covers. Kudzu was amazing. It could grow in poor soil conditions and was protein rich. It could grow at an astonishing rate and seemed to solve so many problems of both farmers and land developers. By the mid-1940s, kudzu had been planted on nearly half a million acres.

By the mid-1950s, the story on kudzu took a decided turn. Engineers and foresters were noticing that kudzu didn't seem to have an *off switch* and tended to consume everything in its path, both on the ground and even in the sky. Kudzu was taking over and engulfing pine trees, telephone poles, empty fields, hillsides, and even the occasional car left unattended for the summer. Today, kudzu is seen as a pervasive, difficult-to-eliminate weed that, left unchecked, will wreak havoc on everything around it.

The story of kudzu is very similar to urgency. In small and proper doses, urgency is a great motivator. However, left unchecked, it can be all-consuming, ignoring stop signs, work/life boundaries, and other pleas for relief.

When I teach classes related to leading or managing change efforts and we discuss the idea of urgency, I always pose the following question:

> *When you feel urgency, what does that feel like? What word or words would you use to describe that feeling?*

Inevitably, I get the following words or phrases shouted back at me:

- Pressure
- Stress
- Anxiety
- Overwhelmed
- High energy
- Need to do something (not really a feeling, but OK)

As the shouting begins to wane, a lone soul or two then might add in the following words or phrases:

- Focused
- Excitement

Most of the words or phrases associated with urgency have a negative connotation.

But then we get those few words like focused and excitement that reminds us that urgency isn't always such a bad thing. So, what is it? Is urgency good or bad?

Why We Don't Like Urgency

For most of us, when we think of urgency, we think of someone or something that has a hand on the middle of our back and is pushing firmly to get us to move more quickly than we would like. It is not a good feeling. For many of us, urgency represents a loss of control. Other people or events are directing our attention and our pace.

Consider the following examples:

The Demanding Boss

Jamal was an MBA student of mine several years ago. After graduating, he took a job with a well-known insurance company. Immediately, he was recognized as a superstar and was fast-tracking up the corporate ladder. As typically happens in that season of one's career, work wasn't the only thing that was growing. Jamal and his wife, Janetta, welcomed their first child. Things were great, except for one factor: Jamal's boss. Jamal's boss had been with the company for nearly fifteen years. She was a director and aspired for more. Her aspirations crowded out most everything else in her world, personally and professionally. Work was her focal point. Everything work-related was urgent to her and she expected her direct reports to feel that same sense of urgency, warranted or not. One day, I got a phone call from Jamal and he relayed the following story to me:

> It was 6:30 p.m. and I was heading home on a Friday. My wife and I had plans to go out that evening to celebrate our anniversary. On my way home, my manager calls and tells me that she is working on a strategic plan that she wants to get to one of our SVPs over the weekend. She needs me to drop everything to work on this plan so she can get it over in the morning. Did I mention it was Friday when she was calling me? I knew it was going to be an all-nighter. But worse, I was going to have to cancel my dinner with my wife. I was not looking forward to that conversation.
>
> Naturally, I gently pushed back on my boss. I attempted to reason with her explaining I had an important family

commitment. When I questioned her as to whether this was really something that required an all-nighter, her response was the same as it always is (this was not the first time I had tried to reason with her): "If you don't make my request the most important and urgent item in your life, then maybe this isn't the right place for you."

I can't tell you how many all-nighters I have pulled in my current role. Everything seems urgent all the time.

Ouch. I'm sure many of us have found ourselves in similar situations. Someone else makes their problem, our problem. Unfortunately, bosses are notorious for pushing their anxiety and urgency down to all their direct reports. They want others to feel what they feel, regardless of how it may impact others. They want others to feel the heat. It is the equivalent of a someone taking a big bite of a spicy pepper, and as their eyes are tearing up and they gasp for air, they insist that you take a bite of the same pepper as well. Who wants to be on the receiving end of that?

Late For The Meeting

Sometimes life events create that unpleasant sensation of urgency. Have you ever been in a meeting that has run late only to realize that you will not make your next meeting across town unless you leave *right now*? I had a similar experience several weeks ago. I had a session I was conducting at a client site for a group early in the morning. The session was scheduled to start at 8 a.m. I don't know what I was thinking that day, but I seemed to be moving very leisurely as I got ready that morning. I hit the snooze button a few times, and comfortably made my way through my morning routine. I hopped in my car at 6:55 a.m. and started the journey through traffic. At 7:40 a.m. I realized that I was in trouble. I had just made it to the highway and based on the GPS's calculations, I was going to be late. There is nothing worse than seeing the *estimated time of arrival* on the GPS gradually creep later and later. 8:05 a.m.... 8:06 a.m.... 8:07 a.m.... I could feel a sense of urgency increasing at an alarming rate. What was I going to do? What was everyone going to think? My fingers wrapped around the steering wheel tightly. I was going to be late and there was nothing I could do about it, and yet, I couldn't get the feeling of intense urgency to dissipate. I was in damage control mode. *If I can just keep my tardiness under ten minutes, then it won't be all that bad.* I texted my client and eventually picked up the phone and called her. With an incredibly apologetic tone, I said, "Ann, I am so incredibly sorry. I am going to be arriving closer to 8:25 a.m. I know we were supposed to get started at 8 a.m. Let's talk about what we can do to still make it a meaningful experience for the participants." After a long awkward pause, Ann responded. "Brandon, we aren't scheduled to start until 9 a.m."

The urgency associated with running late is not a pleasant one. It conjures up fear and worry about what others will do to us as a result of our tardiness. Will they think less of me? Will I get punished? Could I get fired? Our minds spiral with thoughts of catastrophic possibilities. This form of unpleasant urgency is tricky. On the one hand, one can easily make the argument that we can control this. "Brandon, if you had just gotten your butt out of bed thirty minutes earlier, none of this would have happened." Touché. On the other hand, organizations have everyone so over-scheduled (primarily with meetings) that this may be more systemic. I can't tell you how many clients I have that are either in back-to-back meetings all day or have no control of their calendars. When we talk about creating a buffer, they respond, "Even if I put a buffer on my calendar, in my organization, it is commonplace that people will schedule right over it." It feels like a constant hot sauce drip every hour. It is important to note that there is one distinguishing difference between stress and urgency. Stress is pressure. Pressure to get something done. Pressure to get something done the right way. Urgency is stress plus intense speed. Urgency says, *get it done, get it done the right way, and get it done faster. You are already behind.*

Fire At Home

If you have joined the ranks of homeownership, then you are quite familiar with this form of unpleasant urgency. Simply put, this is when *stuff* unexpectedly breaks, always at the most inconvenient times. Dishwasher, washing machine, lawn mower, garage door, and more. I have been a homeowner for almost twenty years and, honestly, I can't think of one of those years when we didn't have an urgent fire pop up. So, I'll just think back to the most recent.

This past July, we were going through a few weeks of sweltering heat, not an uncommon occurrence for Atlanta, Georgia. When we get this kind of weather (with a nice unhealthy dose of humidity mixed in), everyone walks around in a perpetual state of sticky. You open your car door, sit down, and immediately your shirt is sticking to your back. Sweat begins to drip off your brow within minutes of walking outside. Naturally, the last thing we would want to see break down would be air-conditioning. Our air-conditioner met its untimely death in the middle of the heat wave. Talk about urgency. Now, not only were we sweating during the day, we spent the entire evening in a house that felt very much like a sauna. And, of course, to repair the air-conditioner, it required parts that were out-of-stock. Those two weeks were a steamy blur.

Life brings us fires that we must attend to as urgently as possible. The only thing predictable is that they will be unpredictable and unavoidable.

An Agent Of Worry And Fear

We often associate urgency with worry and fear. It can trigger in us deep feelings of anxiety followed by thoughts of doom and gloom:

When is my boss going to make that last-minute request?

Will I get fired if I don't meet the deadline?

How am I going to fix this unexpected problem?

When is another unexpected fire going to start?

Am I going to die?

Living with perpetual urgency as a copilot in life does not make for a fun journey. No wonder that we see such a pervasive use of anti-anxiety medication.

Urgency is an uncomfortable thing.

Why We Need Urgency

Up to this point, we've spent most of this book outlining the many drawbacks to urgency. We have painted a picture of urgency as an unpleasant, intense thing that surprises us. It's as if we are strolling through the woods and suddenly out pops a bear. Our blood pressure leaps, we start to sweat, and we quickly shift into *fight or flight* mode. And yet, in this analogy, urgency serves an important purpose. It triggered a level of discomfort so that we could identify a survival strategy.

Imagine if there was no such thing as urgency. You are taking a leisurely stroll through the woods. "What a beautiful day," you think to yourself. There is a rustling from the brush up ahead and suddenly a grizzly bear lunges forward onto the trail in front of you, signaling you are trespassing. "What a beautiful bear," you say aloud as you continue your stroll. You walk directly toward the grizzly without altering your pace. "I've always wanted to take a selfie with a bear," you reflect, imagining the boost such a picture would give your social media platform.

You get your phone ready and kneel next to the very large creature, attempting to put your arm around its shoulder for this once-in-a-lifetime, sure-to-go-viral picture. I think we know how this story would end. Not so well for you.

Urgency helps us to survive. But urgency can be even more than that; it can be a motivator for growth and change.

Consider the following examples:

The Restructuring

Sherry's boss pulled her aside one Monday morning and delivered the news. "Sherry, the company is going to through some restructuring. After lots of discussion, planning, and pressure from investor activists, leadership has decided that all regional leadership roles, like the one you currently sit in, are going to be eliminated next quarter. That's the bad news. The good news is that there will be two new positions at corporate that are designed to oversee the activities in the regions. We would like you to consider applying for one of those jobs."

It took Sherry several days to process the announcement. She realized she had roughly three months until her life was going to change one way or the other. Sherry decided that she was going to apply for one of the newly created roles at corporate, but upon honest reflection, she recognized that she wasn't ready for that job today. "But I could be ready for that job in three months," Sherry thought to herself.

She set out to get herself ready. She hired a coach who promptly gathered feedback from her direct reports, peers, and her leaders. Sherry and her coach identified not only the leadership skills that she could strengthen, but also a strategy for *platforming* her with senior leadership. Sherry set out to make all the changes as rapidly and as effectively as she could as the clock continued to tick. She worked to develop her direct reports so that they could take on greater responsibility. She found ways to restructure her area so that she was doing more of the work of the new role that she was going to apply for. She made regular trips to corporate to present to leaders on the changes that she was making in her region. When the new role opened, Sherry applied and began interviewing.

After completing all the interviews, two weeks passed with no word from corporate. Naturally, Sherry thought the worst, but as she was driving home late on a Friday afternoon, her boss unexpectedly called her on her cell. "Sherry, leadership has made a decision on the two new roles at corporate that you interviewed for. All the candidates were exceptional. The decision process was much more difficult than any of us expected because of the standards set by each of the applicants. In the end, we've made the decision to extend one of the offers to you. Frankly, Sherry, what impressed everyone the most was the recent work you have done over the last three months. Everyone on the committee agreed that your efforts not only to get your group ready, but also the work you did to spotlight what you were capable of in the role, made you a clear choice. Congratulations."

Urgency can help us focus in a way that we might not be able to without it. It can help us prepare for opportunities or challenges that we want. Without urgency, we are likely to default to the comfortable status quo. Imagine if Sherry had had the option to stay in her current role or apply for the corporate role. Odds are, she would have chosen to stay in her current role, convincing herself that she'd be ready *the next time* something came along. Urgency can help us prepare for what's next.

Ready For The Next Chapter

When I met Alisha, she was a partner in a consulting firm and had an impressive resume. She had made her career a focus, and her hard work had paid off. She had been one of the youngest partners in the firm and one of the few females to hold that position. We were working on few small tweaks to her leadership style when she added another goal into the mix.

Alisha shared the following: "I'm thrilled with my career, but to be frank, I feel like my life isn't quite complete. When I'm not traveling, I come home to an empty condo. I always imagined I would be married and have a family as well as a thriving career. Unfortunately, the consulting lifestyle isn't very conducive to dating. That said, I'm thirty-five years old, and I'd very much like to have a family. If I don't make that a priority now, time is going to run out."

So, I helped Alisha create a plan for how she was going make space in her busy life for personal relationships to take root. She stepped down from a few of the non-profit boards that she sat on. She minimized her travel commitments. She began asking friends to be on the lookout for possible matches and joined social groups on the weekends. She started dating. Six months later, Alisha met Tom, and after a year and a half of dating, they were married. Today, they are expecting their first child.

Urgency motivated Alisha to make changes in her life in order to realize the vision she had for herself. Sometimes urgency can set us up for opportunities as in the case of Sherry. Other times, urgency reminds us that the door is closing and if we don't hurry, we won't be able to go through that door again. In the case of Alisha, it was about trying to make it through the door before it closed.

Writing The Next Chapter

I have always wanted to write a book. I take that back. I have always wanted to write a lot of books. Yet, I could never find a way to make writing a book a priority for me. Between growing my business, little kids, and simply procrastination, my book dreams had never become a reality. After several years of trying to make it a priority and failing miserably, I came to the realization that I couldn't do it on my own. I hired a book coach and it was one of the best decisions that I made. Why? Because when I see that I have a call coming up with Cathy, an immediate sense of urgency comes over me. I don't want to show up to one of our meetings without something completed.

Does that mean that I have found a disciplined routine for my writing? Am I getting up at 5 a.m. every day and writing pages daily? The answer is a definitive no. I still struggle with finding the time in my life to write. It is important to me, but not urgent. I needed it to be both. As a result, my meetings with Cathy create a healthy sense of urgency. The outcome? You are reading this right now.

Urgency can help us to prioritize. Urgency can take something that is a back-burner item in life and lift it to the front burner. And sometimes, accountability and urgency can go together.

Sam Had Enough

Sam had had enough. He was in the worst shape of his life. At least 100 pounds overweight with a diet that was filled with fatty foods, Sam felt horrible. Every day his joints ached. The doctor told Sam that if he continued his current path, he was destined for knee surgery and treatment for diabetes. For Sam, his greatest motivation was his children. He didn't have enough energy to go outside and play with them. Nick and Grace were five and three years old. They were active and wanted Sam to join them in their games and on their bikes. One day, while looking outside and seeing his wife and two children chase each other in the front yard, Sam decided he had had enough. He was going to turn things around.

Sam's first step was to set a goal and a deadline. His annual physical was approximately six months away. Sam made his goal to lose sixty pounds before he saw his doctor again. He would reclaim his health between now and then. Sam joined a gym, began attending nutrition meetings, hired a personal trainer, and tracked his progress. Every time Sam began to slip, he would remind himself that he was running out of time and he wanted to hit his goal. He soon fell into a new routine where exercise and healthier eating became part of his life. When his annual physical rolled around, Sam had not lost sixty pounds; *he had lost ninety-five.* His knees felt great and he was no longer in danger of becoming diabetic.

Urgency can help us reset our lives. It can help us refocus on what matters and make the changes necessary to get back to the lives that we had and perhaps lost along the way. How many of us have ever said, "I want to look great by this summer"? If you have ever acted on that goal, it was urgency helping you along.

An Agent Of Focus And Change

Urgency is a necessary thing for us if we desire to continue to grow and change. Human nature is to embrace comfort. We are comfortable in our current job. We are comfortable in our imbalanced life. We are comfortable not doing things that require extra energy. We are comfortable not changing our lifestyle. Urgency says "no" to comfort. Urgency takes the comfortable plate of rice and beans and adds some heat and some spice. It is the hot sauce in life. It challenges comfort by creating states of discomfort.

Urgency is an uncomfortable thing.

And sometimes it is just the thing we need.

CHAPTER 3 QUESTIONS TO CONSIDER

1. What do you feel when you feel urgency?

   What do you feel emotionally?

   What do you feel physically?

2. When has urgency been a motivator for you to grow and change in your life?

3. Which scenario of urgency as an agent of focus can you relate most to?

   Why?

4. How is urgency playing out in your life today?

   a. What are areas or aspects of your life where urgency is a *good thing*—a motivator for action and change?

   b. What are areas or aspects of your life where urgency is a *bad thing*—it is causing you anxiety, frustration, and stress in an unhealthy or unproductive way?

— PART TWO —

LEADING WITH URGENCY

— CHAPTER 4 —
Preparing Your Team

 Kate went back to her office and closed the door. Her office wasn't large. It was just enough space for a small desk, a monitor, and a few shelves for books, folders, and other knick-knacks.

Opposite of Kate's desk was a floor-to-ceiling glass wall and sliding door that looked out to where her team sat. Kate didn't know if the glass was an effort to be more modern or to convey some level of transparency from leadership. Kate didn't really care. In the end, it felt like she was in a fishbowl.

And yet, when Kate was in her office, she felt slightly protected and sheltered from the energy of the office. Kate sat down behind her desk and faced directly out of her fishbowl to where her team sat. And there they sat. The team all seemed to be holding the same posture. Each person sat hunched over their desk and appeared to be fixated on their laptop. No one was speaking and each appeared as though they were trying to focus on their work for that day to ignore Martin's mandate.

Was Martin right? Kate wondered to herself. He did have a solid point. People are capable of more than they may realize. That said, there was something about this situation that was nagging at Kate. She and the team were exhausted. It is one thing to push beyond your perceived limits when you are feeling strong and rested. It is a whole different story to ask someone to push beyond their limits when they are low on energy and motivation. Kate pondered the situation a few more minutes and realized that regardless of what perspective or opinion she had about their current situation, her first step was clear: Kate needed to figure out a way to reenergize her team.

Kate sent an IM to her team and requested that they clear their calendars for a team meeting. Kate watched her team for their reaction to her request, hoping to see some spark. Emotionlessly, they all agreed to Kate's request. For a split second, Kate contemplated taking the team to a restaurant for the meeting, but she thought better. *I don't want to add extra stress to the team by taking up any more time than necessary,* Kate decided. After some negotiating with another department, Kate secured their favorite meeting room and had a catering order placed from the team's favorite lunch spot.

The meeting started off slowly. Team members entered somberly, one at a time. They quietly found a seat, set down their multiple phones and laptops without saying a word. It reminded Kate of the last funeral she had been to. She remembered how eerily quiet the funeral home had been the during the family visitation. One by one, friends and family members came in with somber looks on their faces as they paid their respects. "Is this what the team has come to? A funeral?" Kate thought to herself. As Kate had the thought, she realized that the comparison wasn't that absurd. "If I don't turn things around soon, it'll be the team that will reach its demise as one by one, team members depart."

Once everyone had gotten their food and returned to their seats, Kate opened the meeting. "I know the last few months have been trying for all of us, and frankly, I don't think Martin's meeting left any of us feeling any better. I wanted to bring us together so we could not only talk about how we are doing, but also where we want to go as a team."

Kate paused and looked around the room. No heads were nodding. All Kate saw was a room full of blank stares. Apathy and rigor mortis had set in. Kate realized that she was going to have to go first and share where she was at if she wanted to bring the team back.

"To be frank, the last few months have been some of the most challenging in my career. While I am so proud of what we have accomplished, I have real reservations about the demands that are continuing to be placed on us. I know everyone in this room has been working long days and weekends, and the expectation that somehow this is okay and just part of our job is unacceptable. Personally, not only have I noticed a toll that this pace is taking on my health, I have also had to miss some meaningful firsts in my family. I'm not comfortable missing those anymore, nor am I comfortable sacrificing my personal health to hit moving targets. If we are going to achieve some of the amazing work that I know we can achieve, I owe it to everyone in this room to set us up for success. Going forward, here's what I think we need to do. First, I'm going to continue to push for more resources. While I don't think that we'll likely get exactly what we need, I'm not going to give up. Second, I think we need to be setting the timelines and deadlines ourselves and not allow others to arbitrarily set those for us. Afterall, no one knows what we are capable of more than us. Third, we need to make sure that we are taking care of ourselves and each other. We owe it to ourselves to not only check-in with each other, but also give ourselves permission to raise our hand to ask for help."

Kate paused to let what she had just said sink in and then she continued, "So, what is this going to look like, and more importantly, what am I going to do to make these things happen? I am going to continue to ask for more resources. I will provide you all with weekly updates on this. And speaking of weekly updates, I am going to request that we meet for thirty minutes each week to discuss progress. I know we are already doing this, but I want this to include two new items: the number of hours you worked last week as well as regular updates on projected completion dates so that I have those numbers to manage expectations. Finally, I'm going to be checking in with each of you every week to not only gauge how you are feeling, but also any needs you might have each week, whether they are for personal reasons or if you need an extra hand. That is what I am committing to do for each of you. We are too good and too talented to allow this kind of noise to prevent us from doing good work."

Kate stopped and took a deep breath and intentionally let silence fill the air.

After some time, Sujata, one of Kate's newer members of the team spoke up. "Kate, I know you have been working hard on our behalf. I think what you have laid out is really going to make a difference for us. I will start working on getting you the items you've requested, and I look forward to trying this new approach."

Byron, Kate's most tenured team member, spoke up. "I agree with Sujata. Frankly, I haven't been feeling very hopeful the last few weeks. I've even contemplated looking for another job." Byron paused and then continued, "But this plan gives me some hope. I really enjoy working on this team and working for you, Kate. I'm willing to back you up. But there is a question that I have for you. What do you need from us?"

A smile came across Kate's face. She was bringing the team back to life. Kate walked over to the whiteboard, grabbed a dry erase marker, took off the cap, and said, "I think there is no better time to get started on this new approach than right now. Let's get started."

Preparing Your Team For Urgency

Several years ago, John Kotter PhD, the famous change guru, was asked by a journalist on the key ingredients to a successful change initiative. His first response was to discuss the importance of communication by leaders. Naturally, no one could argue with Kotter's emphasis on communication. But the journalist was savvy. She followed up and pressed on Kotter for more. Without missing a beat, Kotter responded by telling the interviewer that if there isn't the right amount of urgency communicated by the leadership team, there is little probability of success in whatever measures they wish to implement.

As I shared in the previous chapter, when I work with leadership teams, I often poll my audiences about the presence and effects of urgency in their professional and personal lives. In addition to asking them what they "feel" when they feel urgency, I also follow-up that question with the following:

"When you feel urgency, what do you do to cope? In other words, how do you make that feeling go away?"

Common responses are statements like the following:

- "I write a list."

- "I prioritize."

- "I go for a run."

- "I do it."

- "I reach for a bottle of whiskey."

The important takeaway is that urgency stimulates a "do" response. And that is the crux of why this is so important. If we need to overcome resistance to change, we need to start with urgency.

Start With Trust

I want to be clear. Urgency is about creating an intentional state of discomfort. Or, in other words, urgency is about intentionally putting pain in the system to stimulate change. As leaders, this is not normally what we are tasked with doing. Whether we are teachers, doctors, volunteers, parents, or managers, we spend most of our time attempting to relieve discomfort. We are typically tasked with putting out fires and easing pain in the world. If we are to be successful leading others into the unknown and overcoming resistance, we'll need to do the opposite of what we typically do. We'll need to intentionally make others uncomfortable. This unnatural movement is why creating urgency is advanced leadership stuff.

If we refer to our hot sauce analogy, this is where we begin to learn how to use just the right amount of sauce to perfectly flavor our meal. In order to determine how to perfectly flavor a dish, a smart chef will know well the ingredients he or she is working with. The chef will understand how the ingredients absorb flavor and their ability to hold and change with the sauce. This also hints at a necessary ingredient for our efforts to be successful. We must have trust from those that we want to see change. When we make someone else feel urgency, he or she unconsciously asks themselves, "Do I trust this person enough to allow him or her to make me feel this way?" If they trust you, the answer will be yes. If they don't trust you, you are dead in the water.

Diane's Story

Diane was hired as the executive director of a church day school. The school was not in good shape. With a combination of increasing costs and decreasing enrollment, Diane was walking into a potentially sinking ship. She was tasked by the Board to turn things around. Diane quickly set about identifying all the gaps, setting goals for the teachers and staff and the necessary actions to get there. Within a few weeks of arrival, Diane had quickly identified all the burning fires and was ready to right the ship. She held an all-staff meeting and communicated the direness of the situation to the entire group. In addition, she "turned up the heat" by rolling out all the new goals (and consequences if the goals were not met) to everyone in attendance. Diane effectively delivered urgency, but Diane failed in dramatic fashion.

Unfortunately, Diane failed to build trust with the group before she increased their level of discomfort. The average tenure of her teachers and staff was fifteen years. They had seen executive directors come and go. Upon feeling the discomfort Diane instilled in the group, the group decided that they not only didn't like how they felt, but that they were going to band together to overthrow Diane. They ignored Diane's increased urgency and slowly worked their relationships with the parents and the Board to instill a lack of trust in Diane. They used urgency against Diane by hinting to parents and the Board that there would be mass walkouts if Diane stayed. Within six months, it was Diane who was looking for a new job.

Diane's story is not an uncommon one. If urgency is not used properly, and properly timed for that matter, it can backfire on the leader. A classic example is the short tenure of Bob Nardelli as CEO of The Home Depot. When Nardelli was hired from GE to take the helm of The Home Depot in 2000, he quickly set about transforming the business with heightened levels of urgency at every turn. A senior leader who once reported to Nardelli told me that he slept with his cell phone under his pillow every night because Nardelli gave all his direct reports fifteen minutes to respond to any calls or emails. If they did not operate with that level of urgency and responsiveness, they would be terminated. The problem was that Nardelli invested little time building trust with others along the way. By 2007, the majority of Nardelli's relationships had soured and he was eventually invited by the Board to leave The Home Depot. I was told that when the announcement was made internally at headquarters, there was a thunderous chorus of cheers throughout the building. As one senior leader so eloquently put it, "In retrospect, we needed everything Bob brought us, we just didn't need Bob."

To be successful, we must start with trust.

How Do You Create Trust? The Trust Formula

Trust is a simple yet complicated formula. You'll need to put on your math hat for this one:

TRUST = [AUTHENTICITY + VULNERABILITY] x CREDIBILITY

Let me take a moment to break down this formula and its parts. First, let's examine the elements of the formula in a bit more detail.

Authenticity. While authenticity has become somewhat of an overused buzzword as of late, there is still tremendous value in the concept. What is authenticity? It depends on who you ask. In short, it is a realness and transparency. People experience the real you, regardless of setting. To paraphrase Bill George, the former CEO of Medtronic and preacher of authentic leadership, imagine your life as a house. Most people have one room for work, one room for friends, one room for family, one room for community, etc. If you want to be an authentic leader and person, keep your house, but try to break down all the walls between rooms. Authenticity is an open floor plan. That openness translates into transparency for those that interact with us and experience us; that transparency breeds trust. But note that being purely authentic and transparent all the time doesn't always equate to being a trusted and respected leader. It is possible to be authentically a jerk.

Authenticity isn't about doing and saying whatever you want to, regardless of the audience or context.

We might call those people narcissists. Authenticity is more about being the real and appropriate version of yourself based on the context and the needs of the situation. Our next ingredient to the formula will help to ensure that authenticity stays on the humility side of the leadership spectrum.

Vulnerability. If you haven't seen Brené Brown's TED talk on vulnerability, I highly recommend that you check it out. In short, there is power in vulnerability. People feel more drawn to us when we share some elements of vulnerability with them. Vulnerability can be as simple as asking for help or saying you don't have all the answers. It can also take a deeper form by sharing personal stories of hardship and heartache that shaped who you are. Vulnerability for most leaders is the most difficult ingredient in the trust formula to master. Not only does it require courage, it also feels counterintuitive. You are probably thinking to yourself, "So, I'm going to tell my team that I have no idea what I'm doing or how this project is going to turn out and somehow that is going to garner me more trust with them?" Yep. That's what I'm saying.

I was recently working with a large global consulting firm as they began to shift their business model and culture in a significant way. The leaders came out with a very clear vision and picture on how this was going to work smoothly and was, without a doubt, the pathway to success. The rest of the firm, however, was not buying it. As one director in the firm told me, "We're consultants; we do this for clients. We know how messy this kind of change is. We aren't swallowing this perfectly buttoned-up messaging. We want to hear about all the concerns and uncertainties that our leaders have about this dramatic shift. This will help us partner with our leaders and come together as a group."

Too perfect = skepticism. Adam Grant, in his book *Originals*, gives the example of individuals pitching to investors for funding. The pitches that were the most vulnerable and poked holes in their own arguments (in other words, they told the investors all the reasons why they *shouldn't* invest) were those that received the most funding and support.

Another way to increase vulnerability is to share more about who you are and the events in your life that have shaped you. I try my best to practice what I preach. After years of practice, I demonstrate the power of one's personal story to groups by sharing my personal story of my oldest brother's suicide, my battle with a chronic stutter and my struggle with a horrible boss and how those events ultimately led me down my path to eliminate all workplace dysfunction. Without fail, someone in the group will say to me that after hearing me tell my story, they now experience me as "a real person" (as if I wasn't before).

Vulnerability makes us real, compelling, human, and ultimately, more trustworthy.

And while there is value in vulnerability, how much vulnerability to share and when to share it varies by culture and context. To illustrate this point, I had a client of mine several years ago share with me his experience working in Finland as an American. He experienced the Finns to be all-business and very reserved during the first few years of his business relationship with them. It was only after years of working with them that they began to open and share more about their personal lives with him. Just like dating, there is such a thing as too much, too soon. Understanding timing of vulnerability is important.

Credibility. Credibility is not only doing the right thing but doing things the right way. It is being both ethical as well as competent. Credibility can include things like your experience, your accomplishments, and your title. However, it also includes such traits as reliability, dependability and consistency. Others know that when you say you are going to do something, you do it. Most leaders score well on the credibility component of the formula. However, if you were curious how one might get a poor score on credibility, consider breaking promises, failing to hold others accountable and saying one thing in a meeting and doing something different later. I had a former student reach out to me about her challenges with her boss. It wasn't that her boss was a bad person. In fact, the opposite was true. He was pleasant, agreeable, and accessible. Whenever she had an issue, typically he would respond quickly to see if he could help her. The issue was that he disliked any form of conflict which became a problem when she approached her boss about some significant challenges she was having with one of her peers (and one of his direct reports). She presented documented examples of her peer repeatedly attempting to bully her, avoiding doing their work and, overall, just not playing nice in the sandbox. After seeing the many examples, her boss agreed to talk to the individual and address the situation that week. After a few weeks, my former student checked in with her boss and was told "he was still working on it." He had not had the conversation with the troubling employee and could not provide her with a timeline of his plan to do so.

This continued for months until eventually she gave up. Her boss had lost all credibility in her eyes.

Unlike authenticity and vulnerability, credibility takes time to build and only a moment to crash and burn in a fiery heap. It is a good reminder to leaders that they are always being watched for consistency, predictability, and congruence. Do what you say you are going to do and do it in a timely fashion and you are sure to score high on credibility.

Now that we have the three ingredients to our formula defined, let's revisit the formula. Notice that it is a multiplication formula and not simple addition. That is no accident. Consider, for a moment, that it was an addition formula rather than a multiplication formula. It might look something like the following:

Trust = Authenticity + Vulnerability + Credibility

Fundamentally, this more simplified "addition" formula is flawed. It implies that one could have zero credibility and potentially still have a positive trust score if authenticity and vulnerability are present. From our own life experiences, we know that isn't how trust works. In my own life, I can think of friends and family members that are authentic and vulnerable people but have let me down more times than I can count, damaging their credibility in some cases beyond repair. I might still love them, but I wouldn't trust them with something precious or vital (like the keys to my house), nor would I trust their decision-making or advice that they might offer me. Zero credibility is going to equate to zero trust.

Which brings us back to the correct version of the formula:

Trust = (Authenticity + Vulnerability) x Credibility

One of the fundamental principles in multiplication is that anything multiplied by zero equals zero, hence, to my point earlier, credibility cannot go to zero. If we examine the other portion of the formula, we see that there is a bit more flexibility for us. For example, you might score very low on vulnerability but because of your credibility and authenticity, you still have a positive trust score. Interestingly, the opposite would not hold true. I don't believe you can be truly vulnerable without being authentic. True vulnerability will always be experienced as authentic. But the overarching principle holds true. If you are not authentic and vulnerable (i.e. you score "zero" for each), then you won't be trusted. You'll be experienced more like an over-promising politician versus a truly engaged leader that cares about others and is willing to put her or himself out there.

While this trust formula is multipurpose and can be used to not only guide our actions but even predict elections (I did quite a few interviews leading up to the 2016 United States Presidential election), we are looking at it within the context of creating urgency. The point is a simple one: if we don't have enough trust when we add urgency into the system, those we are hoping to motivate and activate will reject our efforts. What can we do to build trust with others? Consider the following approaches to strengthen your trust with your team before you begin to increase urgency:

Communicate your expectations. State your intentions, motivations, and expectations from your team today. I often coach clients to think about what they believe is their "management philosophy"—the values that are most important to them at work and in life (for example: growth, respect, responsibility, accountability, family, commitment, etc.). Pick the top three to five, write them down, and share them with your team. This will help the team not only understand you, but also what you expect from them regarding their actions and performance.

Tell them what you are hearing. When you get out of a meeting with the higher-ups, you need to be thinking about what from the meeting was relevant for your team and share that information with them promptly. Your team will appreciate your consistent and open approach to communication. Stop the rumors quickly and get the lines of communication going. Trust will follow.

Practice authenticity. Be intentional about sharing who you are as a person. Do you love Thai food? Are you obsessed with bocce ball? Do you have a thing for the beach? I have found in my experiences coaching clients and executive teams that people want to know more about the leader they are working for. That said, to reiterate my point earlier, there is such a thing as too much. No need to spend thirty minutes opening a meeting with a long rant about the difficulties of raising your teenager. However, knowing you have a teenager and seeing a picture of that "apple of your eye," on your desk goes a long way in making you a real person.

Practice vulnerability. Perhaps the most difficult for leaders, the ability to practice vulnerability goes a long way in establishing trust with others. This can take many forms. For example, acknowledging what you don't know or asking for help. Consider any of these helpful "vulnerability" sentence stems:

- "You all know your world better than I do. Can you educate me?"

- "I don't know if this will work. That said, I believe that together, we can figure this out."

- "I need your help…"

- "What have I not asked about that I should have? Is there anything you think that I need to know?"

And when the time is right, nothing highlights the power of vulnerability more than sharing more of your personal story, including all the struggles that have made you who you are. Not for the faint of heart, telling one's personal story, as one Executive MBA student said to me, is like "trust squared."

One important note about vulnerability: It should tie back to the individual that you are being vulnerable with. In other words, it needs to be about connecting and done in a way that makes you more relatable. If you make it solely about you, or if you become too emotional, it can backfire. I recently had a male leader that I was working with who took this too far. On his first day of his promotion, he declared to the team that he didn't know how to do this new role, he didn't want to let the team down, and he was feeling overwhelmed. He began to tear up. One of his female direct reports later told me, "I wish he hadn't gone there. I was feeling very uncomfortable in that moment as I'm sure were many of my colleagues." Don't cross the line from professional connection to a therapy session by asking these questions:

> *"If I share this information, will this invite the group to work more closely with me or will it push them further away?"*

> *"What emotion will I feel if I share this and what emotion will the recipients likely experience?"*

Keep your word—always. An obvious practice but a critical one. I had a client tell me that her manager promised her a promotion several years ago. The deadline came and went. She continued to press, and he continued to avoid her. It became clear to her that he made a promise he couldn't or didn't want to keep. Perhaps he had a good reason, but in the absence of that explanation, she sees him as a trust breaker. She's done with him and has begun looking for something else. Keep your word. That commitment and predictability will foster trust every time.

Be consistent. Perhaps one of the more overlooked elements to building trust is basic "consistency." This doesn't mean that you can't change your mind. Rather, it encourages us to identify the things that we don't want to change, and make sure we protect those. Things like core values, character traits, and even meeting with our teams can be tremendous in establishing ourselves as the *rock* that can be trusted. Consider the story of a Chief Marketing Officer that I worked with several years ago. His function, marketing, had received the lowest employee engagement survey results throughout his entire company. When I spoke to members of the team to determine the source of the problem, I heard the same explanation repeatedly. Here's what one of his direct reports said to me: "He (the CMO) is a great guy. We all like him personally. The problem is that when we have a scheduled one-on-one meeting with him to review our progress, ask him questions, align our projects, discuss our needs, etc., he routinely cancels these meetings at the last minute claiming there was a last-minute senior leadership team meeting that he needed to attend. The message is the same for us. We don't matter." Find those things that are important to you and your people and stick to them. It will make their trust in you go up, and more importantly, it will make it easier for them to change knowing the things that won't ever change.

CHAPTER 4 QUESTIONS TO CONSIDER

1. Have you established trust with your team? How do you know?

2. What conversations or communications can you point to that indicate your team members trust you?

3. In reviewing the Trust Formula, what area do you think you need to address most?

4. What makes you think that?

5. What is one action you could take or practice you could establish to strengthen your credibility with your team?

   Your authenticity?

   Your vulnerability?

— CHAPTER 5 —
Cooking with Hot Sauce—Urgency as a Motivational Tool

Martin sat in his fourth back-to-back meeting of the day. It seemed like his calendar was being consumed with nothing but meetings these days. As he sat, he reflected on the days when he used to do *stuff*. It didn't seem that long ago.

He loved the feeling of completing a project on his own or with a few team members. It was why he still refused to pay anyone to take care of his lawn. The feeling of satisfaction he got after working in his yard was what drove him. He appreciated putting away his lawn mower and tools at the end of a long day of yard work, sweaty and smelling like a combination of gasoline and exhaustion but being able to look out and *see* what he accomplished. His glorious yard would look like a finely manicured piece of art.

But today, he just felt exhausted. After four hours of trying to convince his team members that their current pace was not fast enough, Martin could see that he hadn't accomplished anything. Why couldn't the team get it? Couldn't they tell that he was serious? Martin was used to his kids not moving with urgency at home despite his many efforts to the contrary, but these were his direct reports and their teams. What was he not doing right?

The Perfect Recipe For Lighting Fires In And Under People

Martin brought himself back to the meeting at hand. It felt like déjà vu. He was standing at the whiteboard talking about shortened timelines and needing to move faster, just like he had started the day with Kate and her team. And here was the current team sitting in the room staring at him with the same blank stares he'd seen in the earlier meeting.

At that moment, Martin did something not in the script. Martin did something very out of character for him. He stopped. He stopped writing on the whiteboard and put the marker down mid-scribble. He stopped talking. He simply turned and stood in front of the room, staring back blankly at everyone in the room. He felt oddly naked, and yet deep down Martin knew that his current approach for that day was not and had not been working. Awkward seconds passed with no one saying a word. The only audible sound in the room was the squeaking of chairs as participants began squirming in the uncomfortable silence. Finally, Martin opened his mouth and, to his continued surprise, out came something very uncharacteristically un-*Martin*.

"Team, this is my fourth meeting of the day. It occurs to me that I am not and have not been effectively communicating my message to you. My goal is to get you to see the importance of why we need to move faster, but all that I've been seeing from everyone in this room are vacant stares. What am I not doing right?"

Martin paused for a response and noticed how uncomfortable he felt. As expected, the team's response was impassive silence. Just before Martin went back to *old Martin* and continued his script, a team member spoke up. "Martin, I don't know about the rest of the room, but I'm not clear on why we need to be moving so quickly. I mean, what difference does it really make if we get this done this quarter or next?"

Martin could feel his *inner dad* voice trying to come out. *Because I said so*, he thought to himself. But then he realized that the question was getting at something he had not really addressed in a meaningful way. Yeah, sure, the investors wanted the company to move more quickly, but in the end, that wasn't a compelling reason for anyone. Martin realized it basically sounded like saying, "The people who have invested their money with us want us to do more with less and sacrifice our personal lives along the way so that they can make more money." Even he knew that rationale motivated no one, ever.

Martin thought for a few moments and then turned to the whiteboard. He drew two images. Both images were identical. Each image was a blank chart with a horizontal and vertical axis. Next to the vertical axis, Martin put a $ symbol. Next to the horizontal axis, Martin wrote the word "time" and indicated four equally spaced tick marks. He then went to the first image and drew a steady horizontal line that started about half-way up the vertical $ axis. He then drew the line straight for the first two tick marks, but as he got to the third tick mark, the line took a steep turn downward. And when Martin continued the line between the third tick mark and the fourth tick mark, the line went all the way down to the bottom of the chart indicating $0.

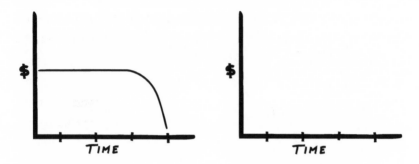

Martin turned around to the room and began, "First, let me apologize for not giving all of you more context. For that I am sorry. Let me share with you what you are seeing behind me. This chart represents the revenue that we get from customers utilizing our technology platforms. Right now, we are somewhere between the beginning of the graph and the first tick mark and each tick mark represents one quarter in the year. Our revenue is steady and good right now. But as you can see once we go from the second to the third quarter, our revenue begins to drop. Why? Because what we are learning from our sales team is that our competitors have already completed their technology upgrades and have been pitching their platforms to our customers to steal them away from us. And guess what? They are getting some traction. Our customers would rather stay with us, and from the conversations our sales team is having with them, we think our clients will give us about a quarter to figure it out. But after that, they're going to start seriously entertaining other proposals. And as you can see, if we wait three quarters, we're sunk. We lose nearly all our market share and find ourselves with barely any revenue left. That doesn't bode well for us. Not a good picture at all. But before you all decide to go back to your desks to work on your resumes, let me talk to you about the graph on the other whiteboard."

Martin moved over to the second graph and began drawing the next image the same way, going about half-way up the vertical $ axis and drawing a horizontal line. The line continued a straight trajectory until it crossed the second tick mark. From there to the third tick mark, Martin took the line in an upward trajectory moving it all the way to the fourth tick mark, where he drew it positioned at the top of the vertical $ axis. Finished, he turned to the group and explained.

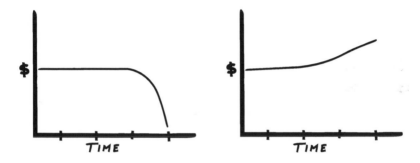

"This second graph represents a very different story. What it demonstrates is what could happen for all of us if we are successful in getting all these upgrades, implementations, and transformations in place over the next quarter. Not only would we be able to retain our current client base, but because of our market position, many of our potential customers would likely prefer to do work with us. The catch is that we must be on par with our competitors in order to get that potential customer business. Our sales teams have said we could easily double our numbers by the end of the year if we can beat our competitors to these deals."

Martin paused to admire his handy work, took a drink of water, and continued.

"So, here we sit here in this pivotal moment. If we can get these transformations done sometime around the next quarter, we can win more customer business which will create more opportunities for everyone in this room. However, if we move too slowly and we wait two or three quarters to get this done, we could find ourselves looking for opportunities elsewhere. Does this make sense to everyone in the room?" As Martin looked around the room, he saw half the room taking frantic notes, and everyone's heads were nodding in agreement. Martin's only regret was that he hadn't figured this out sooner. He knew he'd have some cleaning up to do. Luckily, he liked a good project.

Properly Communicating Urgency

Several years ago, I was working with a well-known luxury retailer. They were reeling from the changes in the retail landscape as e-commerce had fully infiltrated their world. This was particularly difficult for everyone inside this company. In working with them, what I had come to learn is that luxury retail, probably not unlike many other industries, is one where many of the people talk about how they "grew up in the industry." Sure, there may be some company hopping to competitors but, for the most part, no one ever left the industry. Thus, when the entire industry changed, it rocked many people's worlds and their identities.

For generations, luxury retailers took pride in being merchants of high-end goods. They brought fine wares to their customers and they *clerked* with pride. E-commerce flipped all of that on its head. E-commerce became the mega merchant and clerking wasn't going to do the trick. Luxury retailers had to change their culture into one of *clienteling*, a technique to establish long-term relationships. In other words, they couldn't afford to sit back and say, "How can I help you?" They needed to proactively reach out to and engage their customers and say things like, "We just received some incredible shoes in the store that made me immediately think of you."

This was a transformative shift in culture and wasn't easily embraced. There was fear and resistance, but frankly, the company had little choice and the clock was ticking. As one general manager shared with me, "I know I need to light a fire *in* my people, but sometimes, I need to light a fire *under* them too."

Urgency is about lighting a fire under others. Here's how you properly light that fire without burning the house down.

What Is Your Compelling Why?

You may be familiar with author and speaker Simon Sinek and his emphasis on starting with "Why?" While Sinek is, by no means, the creator of that truth, his point is an important one. We not only need a compelling why, but we also need to lead with it and regularly communicate it as well. My belief is that the reason why (no pun intended) this truth has struck a chord today is that with the preciousness of time and heightened urgency around us, we are skipping this important step. Very rarely are we taking the time to articulate the *why* of the project or task before us.

A good why or reason for change should have sound logic and a strong emotional tug. Getting people to change is akin to getting an addict to break from his or her addiction. You won't get there with logic alone. You'll need to throw in a healthy dose of emotional discomfort to get them feeling suitably motivated to act.

Many forms of emotion can work: sadness, fear, anger, worry, etc. As we have alluded to before, there is one emotional lever that has the highest probability of success: anxiety. Your goal is to create a compelling why that leaves others feeling so uncomfortable, so anxious, that they want to do *something,* and they want to do that *something right now.* It's at that moment that they are ready to hear your plan for action. So, how do we establish that urgency? First, consider the following two types of urgency:

Urgency Type One: 'We are going to die... if we don't do something quickly'

This form of urgency is equivalent to laying out a "worst case scenario." It is extremely powerful in shaking people out of their patterns and forcing them to overcome their fears. After all, what's worse than some version of death? With this approach, your goal is to lay out a picture of impending doom. Perhaps that doom takes the form of the organization falling off the proverbial cliff and ceasing to exist unless something is done soon. Or perhaps it takes the form of impending job loss if the individual doesn't change. Possibly, it paints a picture of the individual losing something else precious to him or her (family, friends, followers, etc.).

Regardless of what you choose, this version of urgency entails that you hit them right between the eyes with quickly approaching storms. The trick to creating anxiety and heightened urgency utilizing this approach is to be sure to also attach a short time horizon.

For example, I could say, "You are going to die if you don't change."

In response, you might say, "Well yeah, we are all going to die one day."

However, if I said, "You are going to die in thirty days if you don't change now," suddenly, you are bit more interested in hearing what sort of changes you need to be making.

Occasionally, I must utilize this technique with clients. Consider Tonya (true story, not her real name), a client of mine several years ago. Tonya had taken on a big role that had tripled her workload, and she was not handling her new responsibilities well. In fact, her behavior was out of control: she was yelling at her direct reports, regularly locked herself in her office to avoid distractions, and she wasn't doing any of the actions I had prescribed her. She was failing miserably, and things were coming to a head.

At our next meeting, it finally came time to have the conversation. I said to her, "Tonya, it has come to my attention that if you don't change, you are going to be fired in thirty days. Do you understand what I am saying? Repeat back to me what I just said so I know you know how serious this is."

Her eyes became as big as saucers as the gravity of the situation finally hit her. Change had begun.

One caution with this approach: too much doom and gloom can lead to paralysis. If you tip too far and put it on too thick, it can appear that the situation has gotten too out of control or it is simply too late to take it on. When I get the opportunity to teach this concept in the classroom, my favorite example to illustrate the impact of too much urgency is the trailer to Al Gore's 2006 documentary, *An Inconvenient Truth*.

If you are unfamiliar with the documentary, it details former Vice President Al Gore's exploration of the topic of climate change. I can only presume that the intent of the documentary was to instill a sense of urgency that if we don't move quickly to address climate change, it will be too late.

That said, the trailer is a good example of urgency going too far. It opens with challenging statements questioning the viewer's love of his or her children or love of the planet. It then quickly proceeds into rapidly shifting visuals of catastrophes accompanied by a dramatic movie soundtrack. Images of the past are contrasted starkly with images of the same landscape today showing extreme change and destruction. The storyline is capped off with visual projections of what might happen if nothing is done, showing beloved coastal cities all around the globe submerged.

During the debrief, my classes consistently agree that the trailer's urgency is *too much* and, as a result, ineffective in creating the right amount of urgency. They routinely describe their reactions to the trailer in the following unproductive reactions (Note that my audiences in the classroom range from graduate students to executives):

- "There is no hope. Why bother? I might as well enjoy what time I have left."

- "I don't know where to begin. It is too overwhelming."

- "This is too unbelievable. Where is your data? I'm not buying this."

You may have not expected the last reaction from the list above, however this reaction is important to consider if your audience is highly analytical. If your urgency is *too much*, an analytical-type person will unconsciously activate the logical side of his or her brain to combat the extreme emotional discomfort that you are intending to create. As a result, you will be thrust into *defend your evidence* mode.

A worst-case scenario can be a powerful tool in creating urgency, but it isn't the only tool at your disposal.

Urgency Type Two: 'An amazing opportunity has just presented itself... but we have to hurry'

This second type of urgency paints a vision of great things happening if we act now, but the longer we wait, the more likely it is that this perfect vision will slip through our fingers forever. You often see this approach used when organizations are trying to change their strategy or enter into a new market. Leaders will set out a vision of an untapped market that is a wonderful land of eager customers and high margins as far as the eye can see. But wait, they warn, competitors are starting to pay attention. The time is now to make our move.

This can be a particularly powerful approach if you want to create urgency but not *scare* your audience. For example, consider again my friends in luxury retail. With the emergence of technology in how customers shop, there is an obvious and urgent need to adapt. If we applied the "worst case scenario" approach, we might illustrate the situation like this:

> **Luxury Retail "Urgency Type One" Example:** "E-commerce has completely disrupted our industry. As a result, our customers are no longer shopping with us the way they used to. If we don't adjust quickly, we won't survive and will suffer the same fate as so many of our competitors who have been forced to shut down."

However, if we applied the second type of urgency, the "opportunity scenario," it might sound something like this:

> **Luxury Retail "Urgency Type Two" Example:** "E-commerce has changed how our customers are purchasing. It is providing them more choices and options. The

exciting opportunity for us is that if we move quickly and can meet our customers where they are by integrating technology into our customer experience, not only can we retain the customers that we value and provide them an even better experience, but also it can give us a competitive advantage against our competitors. But we need to hurry. We want to be the first in our industry to figure this out, not the last."

Can you *feel* the difference? Depending on your audience, you might want to *scare* them into action. In other cases, you might want to tap into their competitive spirit to mobilize them.

Which Type of Urgency Do I Use?

Knowing which type of urgency to use isn't quite as tricky as it might sound. A good starting place is to ask yourself this simple question:

Are the people that I'm trying to mobilize more motivated by pain or by opportunity?

Gas Pedals And Brake Pedals

A way to answer the question more precisely is by looking more closely at the function (or industry) in which your people sit. For example, consider this analogy: Imagine that your organization is a car. Some functions (or departments) inside your organization are *brake-pedal* functions and some are *gas-pedal* functions. A brake-pedal function's entire job is to manage risk. They are highly sensitive to, and as a result, are motivated by pain.

Examples of brake-pedal functions include, but are not limited to legal, compliance, finance, accounting, human resources, etc. These are the departments that are tasked with oversight and review. Gas-pedal functions, on the other hand, are designed to propel the organization forward. They are motivated by opportunity and growth. Examples of gas-pedal functions are marketing, sales, research, product development, strategy, etc.

To illustrate this point, I was asked to do a keynote speech to a large conference of leaders who led the *loss prevention* function, for their organizations. In other words, all day long, this group of leaders try to anticipate the latest and scariest threats to their organization. After speaking to the organizer about the type of urgency that would resonate with the group, naturally she firmly settled on "Urgency Type 1" presenting them with worst-case scenarios (she had a legal background, by the way, which was no surprise, given her function). Knowing your audience can be tremendously helpful in selecting the right form of urgency to communicate.

All of that to say, if you aren't sure which type of urgency to lead with, consider combining both. Some of the very best change agents are masters at utilizing both forms of urgency into one message to ensure the message sticks. *Combining both urgency types is the equivalent of your doctor prescribing you a strong antibiotic as well as a steroid to ensure you knock out that nasty infection.* So, consider packing an extra punch by combining both forms of urgency. Illustrate the impending doom if one does not change as well as the potential wonders that await him or her if they change right now. This is a powerful combination to be sure.

While these approaches are fantastic tools for leaders, you don't have to be a leader of an organization to use it effectively. You could use the same approach to get another person to change their role or approach within the team in order to increase their value and importance. I utilize this same approach when I'm coaching young professionals that deeply want to make a career change but are afraid of the change required. I tell them, "My experience has been that if you make this change now, you can have the career you've always wanted. However, I've also noticed that by age thirty-eight, the window of opportunity slams shut. By that age you have family obligations, greater career responsibilities, and a more defined career path that makes change harder. Your clock is ticking so you better move now." It reminds them that there are seasons for opportunity and sometimes you must act in the face of fear if you truly want something.

If You Don't Have Any Data, Consider Telling A Story

In some cases, you might know the right type of urgency you want to use and why you want to use it, but if pressed, you don't have any true data or evidence (at least not yet) that the time is now to make a move. If you find yourself in that situation, consider telling a story instead. Look to another company or organization in another industry that found themselves in a similar situation (industry change, customers leaving, technological disruption, regulations, policy changes, etc.), and tell their story as either a cautionary tale or a tale of hope and heroism. My personal favorite is the story of Kodak.

In 1983, Kodak was the second most recognizable brand in the world. You couldn't go anywhere around the globe where people did not know the Kodak logo. Their brand equity was tremendous, and they dominated the film industry. Fast-forward to the mid-1990s to a time when technology was significantly changing their industry. Digital technology meant that parents no longer had to take two or three rolls of pictures of their five-year old's birthday party, hoping that they got a few good shots. In fact, consumers might not even need to buy film at all if they wanted to enjoy their pictures on their computer instead.

The urgency to change was palpable. Consider what might have happened if Kodak approached this disruption guided by a purpose statement. Reflect for a moment what you believe Kodak's *why* or reason for being was. What was the need in the world Kodak was striving to meet (Note: don't confuse *purpose* with *product*)? You might have come up with something like "preserves or captures memories." If they had used a similar purpose statement to guide their decisions, they likely would have embraced digital technology as an opportunity for them to meet their customers where they were at and get ahead of their competition. Kodak could have used their significant brand equity to propel digital technology and themselves into the future as a household name for decades to come.

But that isn't what Kodak did. Instead, Kodak confused their purpose with their product. In the face of the changing landscape around them, they declared themselves a film company and tried to resist the changes around them with the belief that they were too large, too engrained, and too well-known to fail. Sadly, they were wrong. Today, Kodak is a shadow of what they once were.

Stories of other organizations and the fates they suffered (or enjoyed) can be powerful rallying cries for your organization. Data or not, consider if there are other organizations' stories you can leverage.

Principles Of Urgency

Hopefully, this chapter has sparked a few ideas for you on how you can properly employ something as powerful as urgency in a precise way to motivate and stimulate your group. I will end this chapter by offering several summary principles of urgency to ensure your success.

The messenger matters. As addressed in the prior chapter, the audience needs to trust the person creating urgency. Revisiting the trailer to Al Gore's documentary "An Inconvenient Truth," when I debrief the trailer in the classroom, in addition to the prior comments I have addressed, inevitably a group of the audience doesn't care how compelling the argument is or how well the story is told. They simply don't trust Al Gore. Al Gore, as many career politicians are, is a polarizing figure. If you agree with his politics, you trust him. If you don't agree with Al's political views, you don't trust him. Building on this example, not only do you need to ensure that you have enough trust before you increase urgency, but also you need to ensure that your "lieutenants" have enough trust if you expect them to also be disseminators of urgency. Don't assign the task of creating urgency to someone that isn't fully trusted. It won't play well.

You can't have urgency without a time frame in which to act. The time frame can be three weeks, three months, or three years. The duration of your time frame is somewhat inconsequential.

What matters most is that you have a time frame. Consider slower moving worlds such as higher education, government or religious institutions. In these environments, it is more common for longer time frames, and, in fact, if the time frame is too short it might be viewed as unrealistic. Consider these two different examples of attempts to create urgency in the church world to illustrate the point.

In example one: "Research regarding churches in the United States shows that people between twenty-five to thirty-five years old are not only not attending worship services at a much lower rate than compared to previous generations, but also this population prefers not to commit to annual pledges. They'd rather give if they feel moved in the moment." If we are in the world of church administration, those statistics are disturbing, but it might not necessarily create urgency for our congregation.

Consider this next example to illustrate the importance of including a time frame: "Research regarding churches in the United States shows that people between twenty-five to thirty-five years old are not only not attending worship services at a much lower rate than compared to previous generations, but also this population prefers not to commit to annual pledges. If we do nothing to explore this trend further and adapt, projections show that our congregation will be half the size it is today in ten years. We have fewer than ten years to solve this problem or we will have to make some very difficult choices, including not only what staff and programs to cut, but also whether we can afford the building that we are currently in, the same building that we have been in for over one hundred years." Time frames matter.

To summarize, consider these points:

Urgency is like hot sauce; you only need a few drops. We will explore this analogy in the next chapter in more detail, but the point is a simple one. You don't need to douse your message in so much urgency that it is overwhelming and burns everyone's tongues. That said, knowing your audience can be tremendously helpful regarding how much hot sauce to use. Some audiences only need a few drops of urgency to be uncomfortable enough to move forward. Others need the whole bottle.

The right ratio of urgency to action plan is 10 percent urgency, 90 percent action plan. While this entire chapter (and book for that matter) has been dedicated to the art of urgency, the reality is that you don't need to overemphasize urgency to be effective. In fact, the opposite is more likely to be true. You want to create enough urgency so that the audience is ready for an action plan. This can be just one story, one chart, one image, one quote, one slide, etc. to create urgency. It doesn't take much. It just needs to be used in the proper amount at the proper time, just like hot sauce. We are trying to create productive action, not unproductive anxiety. Hence, we use urgency to set up action, not to take the place of action.

CHAPTER 5 QUESTIONS TO CONSIDER

1. Considering your team's background (function and industry), which type of urgency will be most effective (worst case scenario or opportunity) in motivating them to change?

2. Can you articulate your compelling "why" for change? What is it?

3. What is the time frame in which others need to act?

4. What can you use to support your argument (data, stories, etc.)?

5. Has that already been established with the group?

6. Do you have an action plan ready to discuss with your team?

— CHAPTER 6 —
Dangers of Cooking with Hot Sauce

 Martin left the meeting on a high. He had finally figured out a way to not only get his point across to his team, but he felt like everyone left the meeting *in it together*.

He looked down at his phone for his next meeting realizing that in all of the excitement, he had nearly forgotten that the agenda for the afternoon's senior team meeting was not only to review the current status of key initiatives, but also for the CEO to share an update from his recent meeting with the board of directors.

Martin hurried to the meeting room. He had been trying to make it a point to arrive to senior team meetings early so he could not only have a few moments to prepare, but also to convey a calm collected demeanor to the CEO in an effort to signal that he had everything under control.

Martin's executive coach had recently delivered feedback that people experience him as "overwhelmed and disorganized" when he comes into meetings late. The coach continued that it was hurting Martin's *executive presence*. "Executive presence, whatever that means," thought Martin. Regardless, Martin got the point. He wanted to work on how he showed up. It was a tricky balance. As a leader, Martin knew that he needed to be the "calm in the storm" for his team. At the same time, he didn't want to act so calmly that people experienced him as disconnected from reality.

Martin peered into the boardroom and saw only Michelle, the CFO, seated at the table. She sat motionless with her head down and appeared to be fixated on her phone. Breathing a sigh of relief that he wasn't the last one to arrive, Martin calmly entered and took a seat opposite her.

"Hey Michelle. How are things in your world?" Martin offered. Michelle didn't flinch. She continued to stare at her phone as her thumbs danced rapidly on the screen. After a few more seconds, Michelle put her phone down and lifted her head up to face Martin.

"Oh, sorry Martin. I was finishing up a text to a member of my team. Things have been on fire in my world this week. I've had two team members go out on medical leave and another three team members submit their resignations. Talk about being understaffed."

Martin could totally relate. Before he could commiserate and share his own departmental challenges, like a mini parade, the rest of the senior team filed in. Unlike many teams that Martin had been a part of, this team didn't seem to have any *assigned* seats. People sat more according to when they arrived than for any other reason. Except for Carlos, the CEO. Carlos always sat in the front of the room. After some light chatter, Carlos quieted the group by saying, "I know everyone's time is precious, so why don't we begin."

Martin had always admired how well Carlos ran senior team meetings. He had an agenda, and for the most part, he kept things on track. And yet, he still provided space for members of the team to share thoughts and opinions. Like clockwork, one by one, each member of the team shared a status update on what they were working on. Martin couldn't help but notice that every leader seemed to have as many urgent initiatives that they were working on as he did. "I wonder if their teams are feeling as overwhelmed as mine or maybe they've just figured out something that I haven't?" Martin wondered to himself. Once everyone had finished their report-outs, Carlos thanked the group and shifted the topic of conversation to his recent meeting with the Board.

"As you all know, I met with the Board yesterday to provide them a general update on the status of the meeting. And overall, I would say that the meeting went well. That said, the Board had some serious concerns about our current pace."

Interesting, thought Martin. *I wonder if they are catching on to the dangers of our current pace and are going to help us get more resources?*

After a brief pause, Carlos continued, "Team, the Board feels as though we are not moving fast enough with all of our current initiatives and transformations. They are insisting that we increase the pace of urgency throughout the organization and accelerate all of our timelines."

The silence in the room was deafening. Martin felt like the air was slowly being sucked out of the room. It felt difficult for him to breathe. *What am I going to do? There is no way I can go back to my teams and say, "go faster!" My teams will likely submit their resignations on the spot,* thought Martin.

No one in the room said anything as everyone seemed to be experiencing the same inner crisis as Martin. Finally, Michelle broke the silence. "Carlos, I hear what you are saying. That said, my team has just lost several key contributors, and what you are asking may prove very challenging. What are the priorities that we need to focus on right now? From your perspective, what requires the most urgency?"

Martin couldn't have been more thankful for Michelle. That was exactly what he wished he had had the courage to ask.

Carlos scanned the faces around the table to see if he could gauge others' reaction to Michelle's question. Unable to read the room, Carlos plowed ahead. "Michelle, I hear you, and I am particularly sensitive to your current situation. However, I can't stress enough to everyone in this room that we are *all* behind. After my time with the Board, they stressed that they had expected us to have already completed half of the initiatives that are still underway. So, to your question, what do we need to prioritize? The answer is everything."

The room went silent and the remaining oxygen was gone. One by one, each team member rose and left the room.

Cooking Wisely

There once was a local neighborhood restaurant that had been in business for over fifty years. Like many restaurants with such a long history, it had a humble beginning. It began with an immigrant family that longed for the food of their home country. The parents started serving meals out of their house to share with friends and neighbors a taste of their culture. Soon they expanded to a small location that was barely big enough to seat a dozen patrons at a time. Almost overnight, the tiny restaurant was booked solid with people clamoring for a reservation.

Over the years their children joined the parents in the kitchen, and they expanded to a larger location. Their restaurant reached local fame and was regularly written up as a "must see" destination for locals and tourists alike. If you were lucky to get a table on a Friday night, you would be greeted in the lobby with countless black and white photographs of all the famous people who had paid a visit over the years. The restaurant's tale was a story of years of success that came from hard work, focus, and not straying from the tried and true recipes that had been handed down from generation to generation.

Then one Friday night, something that had not happened in decades happened. The dining room wasn't full. The next night, the same thing happened. For weeks and months, the owners saw the same trend continue. Little by little, customers were coming less and less. The family started to become nervous. What they had always done was no longer working. They heard stories of other restaurants closing their doors after decades of successful operation. They read of customers wanting a different *experience* when they dine. They saw the emergence of technology into everyone's everyday lives.

They realized they were going to have to evolve if they had hopes of their cherished family business seeing another fifty years.

The owners had a meeting to discuss the state of the business. They emerged with several new priorities. They pushed the staff to send food out of the kitchen faster at a pace the staff had never done before. They raised their quality standards to unprecedented levels. Mistakes were not tolerated. But, perhaps their most fateful decision came with the menu. To create a more intense experience for their customers, they increased the spiciness of all their dishes. To unprecedented levels. The result was an unsustainably intense experience for everyone. Staff were stressed every evening. Customers were overwhelmed with the changes. From the staff to the customers, there was plenty of burnout and more than several burned tongues. The owners' panic resulted in dousing everything with hot sauce. The result was failure.

Are You Covering Everything With Hot Sauce?

Most leaders fail at mastering urgency. They operate much like the owners of the restaurant in the story that I shared. Their panic, fear, and pressure from stakeholders result in them dosing everything in hot sauce. The saddest part of the story above (and that of most leaders) is that they have no idea that they are accelerating their own demise. They leave boardrooms patting themselves on the back and saying to themselves, "We have just created urgency in the organization. That is good. We need to be more urgent as an organization. We've done well and are leading effectively."

But really, they're not.

The Three Ways Leaders Misuse Hot Sauce

Specifically, there are three common traps that I see nearly all leadership teams falling into today. These traps are industry and regionally agnostic. It doesn't matter what you do or where you live in the world. I see these traps as pervasive as a virus.

Everything is urgent, all the time.

From big, publicly traded companies to small non-profits, this is a common leadership misstep today. Granted, there may be many parts of the business that are behind, but that is no excuse to make everything urgent. Why is this such a bad thing? Just like our restaurant story, what's coming out of the leadership kitchen is suddenly all doused in hot sauce. The organization members run hard to keep up, but ultimately are overwhelmed. In the organizations I encounter, people are all working long hours. When I ask, "Why are you working so many hours?" the common response is, "There is just too much that needs to get done right now." Ultimately, when everything is urgent, all the time, the result is apathy, lack of full engagement, and eventually burnout.

Nothing is prioritized.

Most leadership teams not only make everything urgent, they also fail to prioritize initiatives. They essentially say, "Do all of these things, right now. We are already behind." This creates unnecessary anxiety in the everyday manager because not only does he not know what to focus on, he is forced to guess and hope that he is guessing right. Of course, his director doesn't know what is prioritized because she was given the same marching orders, so she is suffering from the same anxiety. And rather than forcing her leaders to prioritize, she just relays their call of action and forces her organization to do everything now. The result? No real progress in any meaningful way. Here's a good analogy. Let's say you had a friend who was in very poor health. If they don't get their life healthy soon, they won't be with us much longer. They need to eat healthy, eat less, exercise daily, cut back on watching television, get more sleep, and ultimately lose hundreds of pounds. What if you said, "Tomorrow you are going to eat 50 percent less than you normally do, eat only healthy options, exercise for ninety minutes with a combination of cardio and weight training and no more Netflix. Oh, and you are going to bed two hours earlier." What do you think your probability of success might be? Will your friend be able to make all the changes simultaneously and effortlessly? Doubtful. However, if you said, "Our first step is to get you active. Everything will flow from that. Here's our plan. Tomorrow, you and I are going for a thirty-minute walk." I think your probability of success just went up.

Leaders allow their own anxiety and panic to affect the organization.

Show me a leadership team at any Fortune 500 company, and I will show you a group of exceptionally anxious and worried individuals. Why? Because not only has the landscape around almost all organizations changed rapidly in recent years (and continues to do so), but also the voices of stakeholders are applying unrealistic or misaligned expectations on leadership. Leadership teams are being tasked with innovating their businesses overnight and delivering stellar profits by the end of this quarter, then exceed those results next quarter, etc. Even that simple statement is tremendously flawed. Innovation takes time, investment, and patience. Yet, if it is a publicly traded company, analysts and shareholders aren't interested in patience or waiting for results. They want results tomorrow. Hence, leaders are put into an impossible bind. This impossible bind creates heightened anxiety and worry into their planning and strategy discussions.

Here's where it becomes problematic. Most leadership teams push all that anxiety and worry down into the system in the name of *healthy urgency*. In a sense, they are saying, "The organization needs to feel what I/we are feeling." Yes, sort of. The problem is twofold. First, there is a growing body of research studying the contagiousness of emotions in the workplace. (If you'd like to learn more, I did a TEDx talk on the subject. You can view it at https://theworkplacetherapist. com/tedx-are-emotions-contagious-in-the-workplace/).

What researchers have found is that, yes, emotions are contagious in the workplace. In addition, not all emotions are equally contagious. Negative emotions are the most contagious in the bunch. In addition, catching an emotion at work is not like catching a yawn. It is more like catching a virus. You get it, keep it, then pass it on to others. Finally, the role of leaders is a critical one in impacting the emotions of an organization. What they feel will trickle down into the organization. While yes, it is good for an organization to have urgency, a pervasive feeling of fear and panic isn't healthy for anyone. Leaders need to be conscious of the pervasive tone of their organization and conscientious about how the emotional atmosphere is affected by them.

What Leaders Can Do To Manage Urgency

The good news is that the antidote for leaders isn't that complicated. It just requires awareness and intentionality. For leaders to manage urgency properly and ensure the right amount of hot sauce is leaving their "leadership kitchen" requires the following:

Be aware of what you are feeling.

Leaders and leadership teams would be wise to end strategy conversations by honestly evaluating how they are feeling, where those feelings are coming from, and how those emotions are impacting the decisions that they are making. Below are a few simple questions that, if every leadership team meeting ended with these, would have tremendous positive impact on the level of anxiety in the organization:

- On a scale of 1–10 (1 = low, 10 = high), how anxious are we feeling about the short and long-term future of the organization?

- Where is our anxiety coming from (e.g., analysts, shareholders, competitors, customers, regulations, etc.)? How influential do we want those sources of anxiety to be in our decision-making?

- Is our anxiety impacting our decisions about the organization? If so, how can we ensure that it doesn't overwhelm the organization and prevent forward progress?

- How are you arriving to this meeting? A colleague of mine shared this simple prompt with me a few months ago and I love it. Before the start of a meeting, he asks all attendees to go around and share *how they are arriving*. Amazingly, one hears the stress (professional and personal), anxiety, pressures, and distractions on the group's mind. It allows the meeting to be managed knowing the *operating systems* that are occurring behind the scenes.

By asking these questions, leadership teams not only gain clarity and self-awareness on how they are feeling, but also determine whether they want that feeling to spread throughout the organization. These questions also hint at another important component in this equation: who is behind the anxiety leadership is feeling? For example, leadership may decide that while they want to listen to analysts, shareholders, and other outside but related groups, the urgency that they are applying on leadership may not be aligned with the long-term future and health of the organization. Or, perhaps leadership realizes that the anxiety is coming from competition. This may encourage leadership to ask themselves, "How can we keep an eye on the competition without allowing their actions to dictate ours?"

Leadership is about processing all the noise (emotional and otherwise) surrounding any organization and filtering what matters so that strategic decisions can be made.

Try these actions:

Prioritize initiatives.

Lay out all the initiatives that you would like to see accomplished over the next year. Now, prioritize *and* order all of the items on your list. Assign dates and deadlines to each initiative, if you can. A word of caution: try to refrain from saying, "Well, these can be done at the same time" if the same group or groups are being impacted. If you want people's best efforts, give them the space to focus on one initiative at a time. If leadership does this simple (yet difficult) task, imagine the everyday manager going to his or her director and asking what to focus his or her team's efforts on over the year. Rather than responding with "Everything," the director can now respond by saying, "In addition to keeping up with all of your team's typical workflow and demands, the big push from leadership is to focus our efforts on X initiative over Y period of time. Let's meet regularly to talk about our progress on that initiative and how I can support you and your team in getting this done."

Several years ago, my family and I moved into a house that was somewhat of a fixer upper. While excited about what the future could hold, I was impatient in the *now*. I wanted everything done all at once. And when I say everything, I mean *everything*. Renovate the entire inside of the house, replace the front porch, and demo and rebuild the deck in the back yard. Landscape all the backyard and front yard. Then the time came to make decisions based on what we could afford. Quickly, we had no choice but to prioritize based on the resources at our disposal. Four years later, the inside renovation is nearly complete, and the backyard has grass. However, the porch is ailing, the deck is sadly in need of work and other nagging eyesores still bother me daily.

Prioritization requires a focused use of resources and patience. That's what makes it so hard.

Focus your use of hot sauce.

If leaders are both aware of their own anxiety and are prioritizing initiatives for the organization, they are ready to bring out the hot sauce and apply urgency on what needs to get accomplished. To do this in the best way, consider the methods of another organization that deals with uncertainty, countless threats, and a clear sense of urgency: the armed forces. Most organizations have the luxury of knowing that if things don't go well, no one will die. That is not the case with The United States Army. In organizations like this, there is an even greater call for focused urgency to ensure forward and aligned momentum.

But the Army wasn't always a master of this skill. As a retired military leader shared with me, after the War in Iraq, the Army realized that their traditional top-down method for communicating wasn't going to work in the growing complexity of the world today. The Army shifted how they gave commands to a process called "Commander's Intent." Simply put, when there is a new mission or objective, the commanding officer calls a meeting with their direct reports and their direct reports' direct reports (two levels down). During that meeting, they issue "Commander's Intent" which is the *why* of the mission, the *what* of the mission, and the *when* of the mission.

By clearly articulating your Commander's Intent (with emphasis on the why), you too can keep your troops moving forward with urgency, alignment, and precision.

Note that the commander stays away from the *how* of the mission. There are too many variables and unpredictable elements on the battlefield today to define the *how*, but if everyone leaves the meeting aligned on *the why, what, and when*, they will move forward together. And, after all, in the military they have a principle called *bias for action*.

CHAPTER 6 QUESTIONS TO CONSIDER

1. In what ways is your organization like the story of "the once successful restaurant" in the beginning of the chapter?

2. In what ways do you have to change the ways you do things, as an organization?

   What are the urgent initiatives that need to get done this year?

3. Do you suffer from receiving too much hot sauce from those who lead above you?

4. Are you aware of and honest about how you are feeling?

5. How can you manage this so that it doesn't negatively impact your team?

6. Are you guilty of putting hot sauce on everything or do you regularly prioritize?

7. Does everyone on your team know your "Commander's Intent"?

   How can you regularly communicate that?

— PART THREE —

PROTECTING YOURSELF AND YOUR TEAM FROM GETTING BURNED

— CHAPTER 7 —

Protecting Yourself And Your Team From The Heat

 Kate was back in her fishbowl. Her lunch meeting had been considerably more productive than she could have ever anticipated. In addition to laying out a plan for going forward, the team was successful in getting her everything she needed to present a more compelling case to Martin. When she reviewed the data, Kate was astonished to discover each of her team members had been averaging close to seventy hours a week for months. This included twelve-hour days during the week and at least one full day on the weekend. No wonder Amanda had made the decision to leave. Looking at the numbers, Kate realized she'd had no idea that the team was being pulled in so many directions. In addition to the major transformational projects that they had been tasked with accomplishing, the team was regularly getting requests from other departments to work on their pet projects. To provide superior service, no member of her team was comfortable with telling any customer "no." As a result, the team would quietly take the extra work on and add it to their list of projects.

As more and more of these stories and examples were shared from her team, Kate was shocked that she could literally see the physical, mental, and emotional toll it was having on her team. *No more*, Kate thought to herself. This was coming to an end today. After collecting real-time updates on the status of projects as well as the hours worked from the team, Kate also anointed herself with a new role on the team. In addition to the leader, from now on, Kate was going to function as *air traffic controller* for all projects and requests. Whenever a team member received a request from anyone, whether from an internal customer or the CEO, they were to politely acknowledge the request and then immediately redirect the requestor to Kate for proper scoping, prioritizing, and cueing of the project. Further, Kate instituted a work-from-home policy as a pilot for her team. Her only requirements were the following:

Kate's Work-From-Home Policy

1. Every team member can work from home one day a week; you choose the day.

2. Members of the team need to coordinate so no more than two team members are working from home on any given day.

3. Mondays are a required day for being in the office so the team can meet to discuss status of projects, key priorities, and other needs for the week.

The only item the team was unable to fully accomplish in the meeting was the proper prioritization of all the initiatives on their plate. Kate was going to need to speak with Martin about that. She grabbed her phone and sent Martin a text. "Hey, do you have twenty minutes for us to meet today? I want to follow-up on our meeting this morning."

Kate was still holding her phone when she got a response. "Absolutely! I've been meaning to circle back with you about the meeting so timing couldn't be more perfect. Would 4 p.m. work?"

When Kate showed up to Martin's office, she could see that he was on the phone. He looked a bit more tense than usual. Martin waved Kate in and motioned that he was only going to need one more minute. As Kate was getting settled, Martin wrapped up his call.

"Kate, I am so glad that we are able to reconnect today. I realized that I probably could have done a better job this morning conveying the importance of the heightened urgency and I want to remedy that."

Before Martin could continue, Kate responded, "Martin, I had a very productive meeting with my team this afternoon, and I want to update you on some of the decisions that came out of the meeting. In addition, we need your help."

That last line caught Martin's attention. *They need my help? That's probably the right place for us to start*, Martin thought to himself.

"Okay Kate. Why don't you start?" Martin invited.

Kate then proceeded to fill Martin in on the conversations that she and her team had had over lunch. Martin listened intently. He couldn't help but notice several different thoughts cross his mind as Kate filled him in on some of details. First, he was surprised at the sheer number of hours that Kate's team had been working. *How can I dare ask these people to work any harder?* he thought to himself. Second, Martin couldn't help but to be impressed with how Kate handled the situation with her team. She had created a structure, process, and plan to shield them from much of the daily noise and to help them to manage their priorities and energy. Impressive.

After Kate seemed to finish her update, Martin responded, "Kate, this all sounds fantastic. I'm anxious to hear how it goes. You mentioned that you and your team need my help. I'm happy to help, but it looks like you have everything well under control."

"I'm glad you asked, Martin," Kate replied. "There is one area that we were unable to fully define and that is our key priorities. We have limited resources. We think we can step up our pace, but only if we have a clearly defined set of priorities."

Déjà vu, Martin thought. Instantly, he recalled Michelle's conversation with Carlos and the oppressive feeling in the room when Carlos said, "everything is a priority." He didn't want to do that to Kate, and yet, the mandate from the CEO was clear. Martin thought for a moment on how he should respond and then remembered his successful meeting in the afternoon. Like that meeting, he decided he would take a different approach from his typical Martin behavior.

He began, "Kate, your question is an important one. It was made clear today in our senior leadership meeting with Carlos that all our efforts right now are equally important and urgent. That said, I understand that for you to accomplish your goal to focus and protect your team, priorities are going to be critical.

Let's discuss what we believe the priorities should be, and then I want to have a different conversation. Let's then discuss what could be possible if I was able to get you additional resources."

Kate smiled and responded, "That sounds like an excellent plan."

At 5 p.m. Kate left Martin's office with a clear set of priorities for her team, excited to see what they could get accomplished with this level of focus. As Kate walked out of Martin's view, he was both pleased with how that meeting had gone but also nervous about the meeting he would need to have with Carlos.

Martin knew he was going to have to be able to clearly articulate what was possible and what was *not* possible with their current level of resources. Martin realized he would have to hold firm and not allow Carlos to make a request that was physically impossible for their employees.

Most importantly, Martin knew he would need to get Carlos to make the decision to open the coffers and approve additional hiring. By adding the right talent, Martin knew it might be possible to meet the Board's expectations, but without the necessary resources, their possibilities were limited. He would need Carlos to see that.

Martin peeked his head out of his office and turned toward his executive assistant's desk. Fortunately, Jan had not left for the day quite yet. Seeing that she was starting to pack up, Martin wanted to catch her before she was gone. "Hey Jan. Could you do me a favor? I need to get on Carlos' calendar ASAP. Can you coordinate with his EA and get me on his schedule for a thirty-minute meeting? Thanks."

"No problem, Martin," Jan responded. Martin went back into his office to prepare for a very urgent and important meeting with Carlos.

How ironic, Martin thought to himself.

Don't Let Others Control The Hot Sauce

Several months ago, I was perusing Facebook to procrastinate from something I needed to do when I stumbled across a video entitled "Hot Pepper Eating Contest." Naturally, I clicked "play."

The scene was exactly what you might expect if you have ever watched any kind of eating contest. A row of contestants was seated on an outdoor stage. The emcee came on the loudspeaker and announced the rules of the contest. Each round was going to feature a plate of spicy peppers. The contestants had to eat all the peppers on the plate and not drink any liquids. If they succeeded, they would move to the next round featuring an even hotter plate of peppers. If at any point the contestants succumbed to the heat of the peppers, they had access to instant relief: placed in front of each of them was a refreshing glass of milk that would relieve the burn. However, drinking the milk would mean instant disqualification. Getting up and leaving one's seat would also mean instant disqualification. The last man or woman seated would win. Once the rules were outlined, the contest began.

One by one, the contestants began chomping down on the peppers. It was a fascinating sight. The group of players was as diverse and eclectic as the peppers they ate. Men and women, older and younger, different ethnicities, larger and smaller, all trying to be the last one sitting.

In process of writing this book, I have learned much about peppers. For example, peppers are measured on a heat index called the Scoville scale. As the rounds of the contest escalated, so would the pepper's Scoville number. A pepper would be introduced as well as its corresponding Scoville scale, a distinct increase from the prior round. The contestants would then have to consume the newly presented peppers, all the while, still attempting to recover from the last round of heat. Poblanos, jalapenos, habaneros, and ghost peppers all made entrances. Eventually, there were two contestants left: a man and a woman. The man took a few bites of the pepper in front of him, shook his head in an act of resistance, and then went for the glass of milk in front of him. But it wasn't over yet. His female competitor needed to finish what was in front of her for there to be a clear victor. After a few strained swallows, there was a new champion.

If you are like most people today, you probably feel like there is so much urgency at your workplace that it feels like you are one of these contestants. More and more *heat* is being applied to you without relief and no real alternative seems available but to quit. Believe it or not, there are other options available that will not only keep you in the contest, but also keep you in it to win it with a clear, cool head. This chapter is about learning how you keep yourself from getting burned up when others are applying urgency and *heat* on you.

The goal is to offer you practical tools and actual scripts you can use to communicate your needs and expectations professionally in order to protect yourself and your team.

Avoiding Eating Jalapenos, Habaneros, And Ghost Peppers At The Same Time

We've well established that today's workplaces are hotbeds of never-ending projects and spicy emergencies that must be addressed seemingly immediately despite the current workload. How do you avoid another round of increasingly spicy peppers while you are still attempting to swallow what you just consumed? In other words, how do you get your leaders and stakeholders to back off from increasing the urgency and pressure to unsustainable levels? There are a few techniques that are quite successful in managing the *heat* coming your way:

Prioritization.

There is one glaring difference between our workplace pressures and the hot pepper eating contest. Usually at work, we don't get the benefit of being able to finish the peppers in front of us before the next round is presented. If I was to make the rules of the contest more like the modern workplace, it would go something like this:

> *"You will need to eat all of the hot peppers in front of you, but at any point a new plate or plates of peppers can be put in front of you. You must consume them as well at the same time."*

In other words, "everything is urgent, all the time," and you're pretty much forced to swallow. Your challenge then becomes learning how to slow the arrival of the peppers so that you're not overwhelmed. One of the best strategies for managing the heat placed on you (and your team) is to force prioritization with those who are bringing you more heat. This can be as simple as using the following statement:

> *"It sounds as though this new initiative is extremely urgent. I need your help. Here are the other items on my plate that all feel very urgent that I'm already working on. From your perspective, of all these initiatives, what should the priority for me (and my team) over the next (week, month, quarter, etc.)?"*

By having this conversation, you are requiring the person who has just arrived with another plate of peppers—more work for you—to acknowledge the projects you're already committed to and measure it in light of the new work he or she seeks to add.

While simple and clear, unfortunately people don't always cooperate with us. Be prepared for the following response(s) from your leader (or whoever may be bringing the additional plate of peppers your way):

> *"I don't know. They are all urgent. Just get them all done."*

> *or*

> *"You and your team can prioritize what matters. I'm sure you'll figure it out."*

Both responses are unacceptable and signs of poor leadership. Don't let your boss or other leaders abdicate their responsibility to establish priorities and make decisions (the job of any leader). If you get this type of response (very likely, by the way), respond by clarifying what you believe the priorities are and get their approval.

"If it is up to me (and my team) then from my perspective, this is how I would rank these initiatives. Based on this prioritization, this is when each of these initiatives is likely to get accomplished. Unless you tell me otherwise, I'm going to assume this order works for you and I'm going to proceed ahead with this plan."

Put this in an email to ensure that you have documentation just in the case the *heat bringer* comes back to you later and says, "Why haven't you accomplished all of these by now?"

Lowering The Heat Of The Peppers Coming Your Way

As the demands keep coming, one of the opportunities is to reduce the heat of the next round of peppers. In other words, how do we get the next round of peppers to be either equal to or milder than what we currently are trying to consume?

Convincing leaders to reduce the heat being placed on you is not as hard as it might sound. However, it will require that you have some clarifying conversations with them to identify their needs in order to ensure the right level of spice is coming your way.

Cats, Dogs, And Hot Sauce

Consider the story of my client, Alex. Her non-profit helps to rescue dogs and cats and place them in stable homes. She and her staff love the animals and the mission. In addition, Alex is passionate about delivering an excellent customer experience for the adopting families.

One day, Alex received an email from an individual who attempted to adopt from one of the shelters. The individual outlined one customer service incident after another that they claimed had occurred at Alex's facility that resulted in their not adopting a shelter pet. After receiving this email, Alex immediately turned up the heat to *ghost pepper* level. She promptly sent a memo out to the staff outlining how events like this could never occur again. She wanted to "right things" with this upset customer and began to take immediate steps to appease this irate individual. It became a four-alarm fire.

You may be asking yourself, "This makes sense to me. What's the issue?" What if I now told you that this customer had been previously denied by the shelter four times for not having healthy and safe conditions for the animals that she was attempting to adopt? What if you also learned that the staff went to great lengths to accommodate this individual and educate her on what was expected? What if you also learned that this customer had threatened staff members personally on numerous occasions?

This example is a microcosm of a broader opportunity for us. Leaders are moving so fast that they can tend to confuse beliefs and assumptions with facts and reality. What could have been a *garden-variety green pepper* response regarding the importance of maintaining a focus on service despite the challenge of dealing with difficult customers, quickly escalated to a *ghost pepper* level of intensity based on the assumption that this customer's account was correct and that the organization wasn't doing what it was "supposed to do" in that given situation.

So, what can you do when your leader shows up with a plate of ghost peppers for everyone to consume? If you believe that the leader's reaction is off-base, start by clarifying her or his intent in a way that does not do so defensively or suspiciously, but rather in an attempt simply to be curious and learn. Consider the following response:

> *"I completely understand that this is an urgent matter. My team and I want to move on it immediately. So that we can do that in the most efficient and effective way, share with me any background and context that you might have."*

You'll notice that in my response above, I started by acknowledging the *heat* (or feelings) that leadership is trying to communicate. "Why?" you might ask. If you don't acknowledge that the feelings are intense, they will simply increase the heat. I'm not sure exactly what is above ghost pepper, but frankly, I don't really want to know. Acknowledging the heat locks it in place. Now we need to reduce it. The second part of my response invites the leader to share what she or he knows so that you can clarify and amend. Doing this in the spirit of moving quickly will get you a quick download of background. Once you have this information, it allows you to add some additional background and/or clarify needs from the leader. For example, consider this follow-up response based on what you hear:

> *"Based on what I just heard you say, it sounds as though this is the primary issue (insert any additional information, if you have it). I would propose that we address it the following way in order to not only tackle this situation but any future situations. Are you comfortable with that approach?"*

The key to this approach is to take control of *authorship* so that you not only dictate pace but also the proper urgency to share with your team in order to spare them from another round of ghost peppers. If leaders feel as though you get what they are feeling, and you have a logical approach to alleviate their pain, they will often comply. The key is that they must believe that you feel what they are feeling. Their tongue is burning. Convince them that you get it—otherwise, you'll be feeling the same thing shortly.

Sorry Boss. You Can Only Pick One Pepper

A final approach to addressing a leader presenting a new platter of peppers it to force choice. This approach makes the most sense when you have limited resources and cannot physically or emotionally deliver on all the competing demands. Or to put it differently, you and your team can't eat multiple jalapenos, habaneros, and ghost peppers simultaneously. Your leader will need to pick. "How would that conversation go?" you might say. Consider the following:

> *"Thank you for bringing this urgent matter to my attention. My team and I would be happy to get on it right away. The challenge is that we currently have initiatives A, B, and C underway. Moving on this new item right now would mean that we would need to stop or significantly delay one of the others. This is where I need your help. Where would you like me and my team to focus given our limited resources?"*

If we break down this response, we see several key elements. First, an acknowledgement of the *heat* of the situation (so as to prevent an increase in the heat); second, a rundown of other initiatives that have all been marked as *hot*; and finally, reversing the heat by putting the leader in the hot seat by forcing her or him to clarify priorities and to say it out loud. This is not only perfectly appropriate, but also it is a leader's job to clarify prioritization. In other words, don't let them evade the question. They are paid to make difficult decisions more than they are paid to do the work. Make them do their job.

Drinking Milk To Stop The Burn

Sometimes the burn is simply too much to continue to bear. In that case, there are two things you can do to reduce the burn temporarily and give you and your team a respite:

Say No.

This approach can be a politically sensitive one depending on who you say "no" to. That said, saying no is crucial in preventing more plates of peppers from coming. To say no properly, your first step is to avoid all the most popular articles on how to do this *effectively*. They all, and I mean all, have it wrong. Flat out wrong. Here's why: All the articles on this subject seem to say the same things. They encourage you to be clear, state your rationale, and hold your ground. What they miss is that if you follow only this approach, you have inadvertently set up a negotiation with the person to whom you're saying no. In other words, if the receiver of your no can overcome your rationale, they win and you have to say yes. The right way to say no is 20 percent no and 80 percent of you providing an alternate solution. Go into problem-solving mode and find another person or resource to solve the problem at hand. Find someone else to eat the pepper. Here's an example:

> *"I completely understand the urgency of the situation and I agree with you that something needs to be done right away. Unfortunately, neither my team nor I will be able to be a solution for the following reasons. . . That*

said, I do believe there is a good solution to solve this challenge. Here are a few possible options which, given the situation, would be the very best paths forward. . ."

Upon breaking down this response, we see a common pattern. We are acknowledging the heat so that it doesn't increase. Next, we are saying no and briefly (very briefly) sharing some rationale, then we are moving into problem-solving mode. Maybe it is a colleague we are suggesting for the peppers. Perhaps we recommend hiring contractors to eat the peppers. Regardless, if you can find a solution to the problem that doesn't involve you, you have successfully said no. In my humble opinion, this is the only practical and effective way to say no when the heat is being applied.

Sorry Boss. I Don't Eat Peppers Between The Following Hours

A final strategy for slowing the flow of peppers your way is to establish *blackout periods*. This is essential if you aspire for any type of work/life balance. In practical terms, this means establishing times during the day that you will not, by any means, respond to emails, queries, and the like. In order to establish boundaries, professionally or personally, it requires two steps. First, one must establish, communicate, and educate the other party on the boundaries. This will require some rationale, but mostly your firm will and commitment. Consider the following:

"Just so you are aware, typically between the hours of 6 p.m. to 9 p.m. every night, I focus on my family and will be unavailable for phone calls and emails. I regularly log back between 9–10 p.m. and am happy to respond to you at that point."

I had a client of mine several years ago that had a medical condition that required she get ten hours of sleep every night to maintain her health. This was a case when she could legitimately say she had "doctor's orders" to not communicate between the hours of 9 p.m. and 9 a.m. Shouldn't we all get that doctor's order?

The second and final step with any boundary is holding the boundary. To state the unfortunate obviousness of boundaries placed on humans, they naturally test the boundary. You'll need to be ready to hold the line. In other words, don't cave on your boundary—*ever*. Once you cave, it ceases to be a boundary. It then becomes a general guideline that can be bent at the will of the bender. Be firm.

A great example of this is the policy that is being adopted by many consulting firms. Consulting firms are requiring that their consultants do *not* respond to or correspond with clients between 5 p.m. on Friday and 9 a.m. on Monday morning to ensure that the weekend is protected as a time for the consultants to reconnect with their families before they hit the road again on Monday morning. Hold your boundary. If you find that your boss doesn't respect your boundary despite your efforts, that is a sign that you need to find a new employer. Healthy adults respect boundaries. Period.

I Can't Eat Another Pepper. I'm Pushing Away From The Table

Finally, there may come the point when you simply cannot eat another pepper. You are done. The urgency levels are not only unhealthy, but also unproductive. In this case, you have two options to try to fundamentally change the flow of peppers coming your way.

First, threaten to leave. As a reminder, this not a *bluff* strategy. If you employ this strategy, you must first be prepared to leave. Second, you must also have a sense that you are highly valuable (and difficult to replace) to the organization. If you choose to employ this strategy, consider using the following statement:

> *"I want to tell you how much I am committed to our vision and what we are trying to accomplish. That said, the rate of urgency is making it increasingly difficult to manage my team and our priorities. If I can't get more support from leadership on this issue, I'm unfortunately going to need to start looking for other opportunities."*

Note that the statement starts with your commitment to the organization. You are stating how committed you are to leadership and the vision. You aren't blaming anyone (although, I'm sure you would like to). Then, there is a pivot to the problem and a plea for help from leadership. In other words, the path to keep you is made clear and it has nothing to do with money. I'm quite intentional with this. If you negotiate for money instead, know that if you are successful, the heat and rate of the peppers will triple. Be careful what you wish for.

If you want to truly play hardball, you can try the second and final option. Go get yourself another offer. With another offer in hand, you can truly negotiate (urgency *and* salary). Here's how you might want to set up that conversation:

> *"I think everyone here knows how committed I am to the organization and our mission. That said, I think we all know that the last few months (years) have been exhausting with the amount of competing priorities and challenge we have had with remaining focused in an*

environment where everything is urgent all the time. If I was to say this hasn't taken a personal toll on me and my family, I wouldn't be telling the truth. I was recently presented with an offer to leave the company for another opportunity. While the offer is compelling, I would rather stay here and be part of this team. That said, if I stay, some real changes would need to be made."

Note that of all the conversations I have prepared thus far, this one is the most real and direct. Why? Because you have a competing offer. You can play hard ball. If you do decide to negotiate, consider urgency first and pay second to ensure that your *pepper heat* doesn't increase if you stay. Second, get it all in writing. If they don't agree, leave. Know that what contributes to urgency of most organizations today is very thin benches. They need you. That said, be cautious and discerning of where you are going. You might be sold *green peppers* and find yourself in a land doused with the hottest hot sauce imaginable.

CHAPTER 7 QUESTIONS TO CONSIDER

1. How could you encourage prioritization from your manager?

   Have you ever forced prioritization?

   How did that go?

2. Are there times when your manager overreacts and adds too much urgency to a situation?

   How could you use clarifying questions to adjust "the heat"?

3. Have you ever set boundaries by either saying "No" or setting "blackout" times on your schedule?

   Were your boundaries respected?

4. Have you ever seen a colleague effectively manage urgency from their manager?

   What did that look like?

— CHAPTER 8 —
Cooking With Hot Sauce At Home

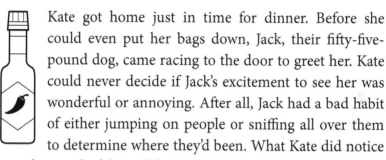 Kate got home just in time for dinner. Before she could even put her bags down, Jack, their fifty-five-pound dog, came racing to the door to greet her. Kate could never decide if Jack's excitement to see her was wonderful or annoying. After all, Jack had a bad habit of either jumping on people or sniffing all over them to determine where they'd been. What Kate did notice was the wonderful smell from the kitchen. Mike, her husband, had picked up dinner for the family on his way home.

"Hey Honey. How was your day?" Mike said.

"Actually, it wasn't half bad," Kate replied.

"That's different. I can't recall the last time you said you had a pretty good day at work," commented Mike. "Grab a plate and we can catch up."

As Kate prepared her food, she noticed that the rest of her family was already seated at the table. *When was the last time we sat down to dinner together?* she thought to herself. Ben, her twelve-year-old, was seated on one side of the table and directly across from him sat his fourteen-year-old sister, Ainsley. Over dinner, everyone shared a little bit about their day. Ben's day was uneventful, at least what the table was able to get out of him.

Ainsley, on the other hand, was obviously struggling with the demands of being a freshman in high school. The teachers were really turning up the heat on the students in an effort get them in the best position possible for college. However, because none of the teachers or administrators seemed to coordinate, the message Ainsley (and Mike and Kate as well) was receiving was that everything was urgent and a priority—from homework, to tests and quizzes, to studying for the future SAT. Kate could see that Ainsley was struggling to keep tears down and keep her voice level as she described her day. Kate made a mental note to check-in on Ainsley before she went to sleep to see if she could help her deal with all the demands and pressure of high school.

Eventually, the kids got up and after putting their dishes in the dishwasher, headed off to their rooms to get ready for school the next day. Kate began replaying the events of the day to Mike.

After she had finished, Mike said, "Now I can see why this was such a positive day. It sounds like you might be onto something. Maybe we can use some of your strategies with our family calendars, because frankly, I'm feeling a bit stressed out with all our commitments. For example, here's what we've got on the calendar for this upcoming week:

Monday. Ainsley: cross country practice after school. Pick-up at 6 p.m. Ben: baseball practice 6 p.m. to 8 p.m.

Tuesday. Ainsley: cross country practice after school. Pick-up at 6 p.m. Ben: math tutor from 5 p.m. to 6 p.m.

Wednesday. Ainsley: cross country practice after school. Pick-up at 6 p.m.; Ainsley: math tutor 7 p.m. to 8 p.m. Ben: baseball practice 6 p.m. to 8 p.m.

Thursday. Ainsley: cross country practice after school. Pick-up at 6 p.m.

Friday. Ainsley: cross country practice after school. Pick-up at 6 p.m.

Saturday. Ainsley: cross country meet. Drop off at the high school at 6:30 a.m. and pick-up from the high school at 11:30 a.m. Ben: baseball game: 9:30 a.m. to 11:30 a.m.

Sunday. Whole family: church from 9 a.m. to 11 a.m. Lunch with Kate's parents from noon to 1:30 p.m."

Mike paused. "On top of that schedule for the kids, I want to get back on a workout routine. I know you do too. I've also been asked to be on the neighborhood homeowner's association to serve as treasurer and the church reached out to see if I'd consider being on the finance committee. At work, my department chair has asked if I would be willing to sit on the curriculum committee for the next year. At the high school, the cross-country team sent us an email to ask if we would be willing to be chaperones for the meets this season. Ben's baseball team is looking for dads that might available to help run practices. And if that wasn't enough, I just got a voicemail message from my brother asking if we would be willing to host everyone at our house for Thanksgiving this year."

Mike paused and looked at Kate with a slight smirk on his face as if to say, "Okay rock star. You figured this out at work. Let's see what you can do when it's really personal and we might have to tell people close to us no."

Kate thought for a moment. On the one hand, most everything that she heard wasn't a surprise. That said, the sheer volume of *stuff* did feel a bit overwhelming. And her work schedule wasn't going to do them any favors anytime soon. Thank goodness Mike had a bit more manageable teaching load this semester at the university.

"Let's do a little exercise," said Kate. "Let's take everything you listed and put them into two categories. The first category we'll call 'Family Priorities.' This will represent our work commitments, taking care of ourselves, and our kids' commitments. This should represent about 90 percent of our activities every week. The second category we'll call 'Bonus Time.' This will represent the items that we don't have to do, but if we had remaining time and interest, we might consider. This category should fill in the remaining 10 percent of our time."

"All right," said Mike. "Let's see what we can come up with."

Without needing much discussion, Kate and Mike quickly agreed that the work commitments, getting exercise (and sleep) and their kids' current activities all fell within the "Family Priorities" category. They worked together to determine when they were going to start working out (Kate in the morning and Mike during the middle of the day at the university fitness center). They also agreed that anything else their kids might want to do, would likely need to go to the "Bonus Time" category; otherwise, they might be sacrificing more important family commitments. They also decided that the curriculum committee could fit in the "Family Priorities" category because it would be good for Mike's career and could be done during regular work hours. In the "Bonus Time" category, they added Mike helping with Ben's baseball team. It was only one season, not a mandatory commitment, and Mike wanted to do it. They also decided to consider the Thanksgiving hosting request, as it would only be a one-time event. They also added to the "Bonus Time" category Kate's small group that meets once a month. Although only once a month, Kate found it rewarding. Off the plate completely went the church finance committee, the chaperone request, the homeowner's association role, and a few other things.

"I think we did a pretty good job," said Kate. "But I just realized that we are missing something in our 'Family Priorities' category: us. We don't have us on the calendar. I think we need to add that into the priorities category to make sure we are being intentional about spending time together."

"I couldn't agree more," said Mike. "What about going out with me on a date this Friday night? I'm buying," Mike smirked.

Feeling good about the evening, Kate was on a high. There was one final question she was wrestling with as it related to her team. How could she be sure that they kept to their set of urgent priorities and didn't let other things creep into the list? Kate realized *the moment everything becomes urgent, nothing is urgent.* She walked over to the pantry and opened the doors in search of a treat she could take up to Ainsley's room to cheer her up.

That's when Kate saw it: the answer to her question was staring right at her and it couldn't have been more perfect—all three of them.

Urgency At Home

Sherri felt pressure. Her stakeholders were constantly telling her what she needed to focus on. The marketplace seemed to be placing more and more pressure on her to develop her direct reports faster otherwise, the outcome was going to be disastrous. Sherri's partner, Stan, felt the same pressure. He felt torn to be in multiple places at the same time. Everything seemed to be on fire.

Sherri had a meeting with her three direct reports to convey the urgency of the situation and the need for them to focus on the tasks that she and Stan had outlined for each of them. As she finished her hot sauce-induced rant, Elizabeth, Cole, and Bryce just looked at each other, not sure what to say. All they knew was that they needed to do their best to please Sherri, but they weren't sure where to start. It felt like everything around them was a swirling pool of anxiety. Elizabeth (eight years old), Cole (six years old), and Bryce (three years old), headed back to their rooms to worry.

Sherri and Stan are parents in today's messy world where time is everyone's most precious resource and urgency runs rampant. This entire book has been dedicated to the toll that urgency takes in our professional lives. These forces affect us in our personal lives just as much as they do in our professional life. And like Sherri and Stan above, what most adults don't realize is that they control the emotional tone and tenor in their homes. They can choose how they react to the hot sauce that stakeholders are trying to apply.

Sadly, most adults (and parents in particular), do exactly that. They react. They eat one pepper after another with the belief that either they'll get used to the burn or eventually the peppers will end. And in the case of parents, there is the belief that if they endure the constant assault of peppers, just like in the case of the hot pepper eating contest, they will eventually "win," with perfect children that have achieved everything that others say is so urgent.

There are many kinds of pressures and urgency being thrust upon us in our personal lives. Consider the following categories of "Life" peppers:

The *Run Of The Mill* Jalapeno Peppers

Just like jalapenos that can be used in so many dishes from nachos to burgers, in our personal lives we experience common *operational* urgency. Examples of this include any of the following:

- Broken toilet
- An aging deck
- Leaky faucet
- Worn car tires
- Paying taxes
- Taking the dog for a walk
- Poor health
- A distant relationship with our spouse

The list could go on. The jalapeno peppers in our lives start with a low burn, but if we don't attend to them in a timely manner, the heat will increase until we have a full-blown Carolina Reaper on our hands. We all know this intellectually, yet how often have you put off attending to one of the jalapeno peppers only to have it suddenly flame into something much hotter? Your tire blows out on the highway. Your deck begins to give during a party. You come home from vacation to find your house partially flooded, or some other disaster.

Guilt Peppers

Introducing a new family of peppers: the guilt pepper. There are many strains of this pepper. The most common characteristic is that the heat is very slow and subtle at first, but over time it increases in a slow burn until it becomes an all-consuming experience. Consider the following strains of the guilt pepper:

Guilt Pepper Familia. This pepper is commonly delivered by a family member. Most often originating from a parent, this pepper is known for its unique flavors of disappointment, unspoken expectations, obligation, passive aggressive behavior, and resentment. Perhaps you've had this pepper before. Examples might be:

- The expectation that you would spend the holidays at your family/in-law's house instead of your own

- The expectation that you would invite and host your family/in-laws at your home and cater to their every need

- Rescuing a sibling or other family member every time they get into trouble

- Having things just the way your mom/dad would want them before they come over

Ironically, *Guilt Pepper Familia* can outlast the deliverer. I know many people still operating with urgency to please a parent that has long-since passed.

Guilt Pepper Volunteeria. This pepper is commonly found in one's community. It often originates from a member of an organization or group to which you belong. This pepper is known for its unique flavors of desperation, disappointment, pressure, and obligation. One of the unique traits of the *Guilt Pepper Volunteeria* is that once you consume one, you are likely to get another with little regard for how many you might currently be chewing. Examples of this strain might include:

- You are asked to be a room parent for your third grader

- You are asked (in my favorite cases, nominated while you are absent) to be president of your homeowners' association

- You are asked to serve on multiple committees at your place of worship

- You are asked to continue to chair the charity event that you have run for the last three years, even though you have repeatedly said last year was your last

Guilt Pepper Volunteeria preys on our belief that we are a bad/selfish person if we do not eat the pepper. Who wants to be a bad person?

Guilt Pepper Parentia. This pepper is unique to those individuals who choose to have and raise other human beings. If you don't have kiddos of your own, you are immune to this pepper. However, if you do have kiddos, this pepper could keep you fully occupied for eighteen years or more if you let it. It originates from other parents, schools, and institutions dedicated to developing children and young adults. The unique flavors of this pepper include such tasty elements as fear of failure, shoulds, supposed-tos, pressure, and falling behind. The entire foundation of the *Guilt Pepper Parentia* is the ludicrous belief that if you overschedule and push your child every step of the way, then she/he will get into the perfect college (Ivy League preferred), and then (my favorite part), life success is guaranteed. Obviously, a ludicrous idea. Yet, parents consume this pepper daily and subsequently pressure other parents to do the same. Examples of this strain include any and all the following:

- Believing that if you push your child to do sports competitively starting at age four, and allow that activity to consume evenings and weekends, your child will surely receive a college scholarship and life success and happiness will be assured

- Believing that your child must play a musical instrument at the level of a master and therefore must rigidly practice multiple hours daily, receive personal instruction and play concerts after their weekend sporting events are over

- Believing that a set number of volunteer activities for your child is critical to any good college application and therefore, you must ensure that this is worked in. You find time doing overnight volunteering at a homeless shelter to not disrupt athletics or musical endeavors

- Believing that any grade less than an A is unacceptable from your child. Harvard does not accept an A-. More tutoring, studying, and shuttling them around abounds

Is it any wonder that kids today report some of the highest levels of anxiety since documentation? In addition, young adults have little work experience by the time they graduate from college (when would they have time?) and have little interest in getting a driver's license (they already have a personal driver). *Guilt Pepper Parentia* is the longest lasting of the guilt peppers, and unfortunately, does not deliver on its promises.

Managing Life Peppers

There is good news. Managing life peppers can be done. Like managing work peppers, your first step is prioritization. This will allow you to know what peppers deserve attention and which can be delayed or avoided altogether.

For most of us, our management of life peppers looks a lot like the classic hub and spoke model used to illustrate how airlines operate. We are in the center and all of the life peppers are swirling around us trying to grab our attention. We tend to eat the hottest peppers first in this model, so, in other words, if a pepper is not too spicy at the moment (think your declining personal health or that worn set of tires on your car), you will delay eating it until something more major occurs and it truly gets your attention. In a sense, we are creating the very urgency that we are trying to avoid. The leak finally explodes in the kitchen. The deck collapses in the backyard. Our spouse walks out.

The first step is prioritizing the peppers, not based on urgency, but based on priority and value in and to one's life. Consider regrouping all the demands on your time (peppers) into two different circles. The inner circle is your most important. What falls in this circle are three main items:

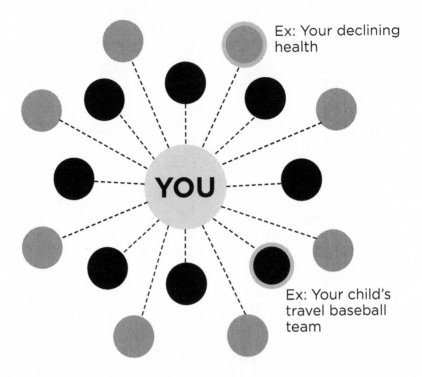

Ex: Your declining
health

Ex: Your child's
travel baseball
team

- Your family commitments (e.g., work, raising children, pets, home maintenance, etc.)

- Your health (e.g., physical, mental, emotional, spiritual, etc.)

- Your partner/spouse (e.g., regular connecting time, date nights, etc.)

This inner circle should be approximately 90 percent of your time. It should get your attention first and foremost. In the classic story of the professor that illustrates the importance of priorities by putting the big rocks in the jar first before the smaller rocks, sand, and water, this first circle represents your big rocks. They should get your focus and attention.

Your second circle is everything else. This is your outer circle. It might contain any/all the following and more:

- Volunteer activities and requests

- Requests from your extended family not living in your home. (Yes, this includes demands from Mom and Dad.)

- Hobbies and interests: yours and your children's. (Personally, I'd put your kiddos' sporting activities in this category, but it is not a popular opinion.)

- Time spent with friends

- Other forms of community involvement

This outer circle should be no more than 10 percent of your time. If you look at the items I have offered as examples, they are all good and worthy things. We want to spend time with friends. We want to nurture our hobbies. We want to make mom happy. We just must be conscious to not let these things trump the real priorities in our life represented in and by the inner circle. And don't be fooled by 10 percent as if it is a low number. If we take a typical week of seven days at twelve hours a day, that is a total of eighty-four hours. That means 10 percent of that is approximately eight-and-a-half hours to offer to the outer circle. That almost feels too generous, if you ask me.

Prioritizing the *peppers* in our life is only the first step. Next comes managing and resisting the inevitable pressure that will come from the peppers in the outer circle in an effort for you to make them a greater priority. The boundaries and walls you establish around the inner circle will need to be clearly stated

and firmly protected. Consider the following ways to establish and communicate those boundaries:

Offer a set amount of time. For example, let's say you get a request to assist with a fundraising event for an organization of which you are a member. You are being asked to be on the core team, and it is pitched as a great honor. After all, they could have picked anyone, but the committee decided you were the ideal choice. (Can you smell the spicy aroma of *Guilt Pepper Volunteeria*?) You are torn. You want to help, but you know that this will be an all-consuming event. You don't want to say yes and let this pepper into your inner circle, but you don't want to say no either. The best approach is to offer a set amount of time. For example, you could respond to the requestor with this statement, "Unfortunately, I can't commit to serving on the core team. However, I truly want to help. I would be able to give approximately three hours on the day of the event to assist in any way that you might need me. Would that be helpful?"

Delegate. Perhaps you are being asked to do something and you have already done that thing and have no interest in making it another urgent priority in your life. For example, your neighbors generously voted you the treasurer of your homeowners' association for the fourth year in a row. You decided, and clearly told them last year, that you were done. Finished. No more treasurer for you. And yet, here we are. You were nominated once again because, in their words, "No one has been near as good in the role as you. You just can't be replaced" (ah, the spicy aroma of *Guilt Pepper Volunteeria*, once again). And then you remember the lovely conversation you had with the new neighbors two doors down. Rather than say no, consider delegating. It might sound something like this, "I'm flattered that everyone was so pleased with my effort the last few years. That said, I truly can't commit to the role this year. However, I had a wonderful conversation with the new neighbors, and I am certain this could be a good opportunity for them to plug into the neighborhood. In addition, I believe she has an accounting background, which would make her a perfect fit. Ask them and let them know that I am happy to get them up speed. It would be my pleasure."

Outsource. Another way to address the pressures and urgencies of the inner circle and the outer circle is to outsource the activities. In other words, pay other people to eat the peppers so you don't have to. This does require resources, but depending on the peppers, this may worth it. For example, consider the couple that want to spend more time traveling (this would fall in the category of outer circle stuff). Unfortunately, they have a house with a yard and two golden retrievers. How do they solve this challenge? They hire a lawn service and hire a house sitter to watch the dogs and the house while they are gone. No flooded rooms. No doggie accidents. No complaints from the neighbors about the condition of the yard. They essentially bought themselves more time for the outer circle.

Say No.

And then there is the simple, old-fashioned approach to setting boundaries: just say no.

This can be done firmly and gracefully. It doesn't have to be a blunt instrument. For example, consider the young couple that has two children under the age of four. For years, they spent every Christmas shuttling between one spouse's set of family in the morning and the other spouse's set of family in the afternoon. Inevitably, each set of family was disappointed in how much time they received during the young couple's visit. On top of it, the rushing around and urgency to please everyone only left the young couple tired and feeling more resentful (Guilt Pepper Familia at its ripest). As the holidays near once again, this might be how the young couple ends the madness: "As we are approaching Christmas this year, we wanted to give you a heads-up that we won't be going anywhere this year. We have decided that we would like to start our own family traditions for Christmas in our home while the kids are still little. That said, if you would like to come over for a portion of the day, we would love to have you."

Track your time and watch your boundaries. Do this and you will not only ensure that you are focusing on the right things, but you will be eating fewer spicy peppers overall. You'll be addressing things proactively before they move up on the Scoville scale. Life will taste so much better.

What If I Need To Increase The Heat At Home?

Most of this chapter has been spent on reducing the heat that you feel at home. However, there are times when you just might need to turn it up. In other words, others aren't operating with the sense of urgency that you need of them. Your kids aren't doing their homework on time. Despite repeated requests, your spouse continues to not do that thing that you keep asking her or him to do.

To effectively turn up the heat at home, consider these two essential ingredients:

Establish A Time Frame. To reiterate a point from an earlier chapter, you can't have urgency without a time frame in which to act. In other words, you need a ticking clock. With your kids, it might take the form of a deadline for them to get something done. Example: "You have until noon on Saturday to get your room cleaned. At that point, I will show up and evaluate your progress." With your spouse, it could take the same approach but delivered a bit more softly. Example: "Honey, we've got a bunch of things coming up over the next few months and I want to make sure we get in front of all of our commitments. Can we set up time to talk about what needs to get done and commit to some deadlines? That would help me tremendously."

Parenting Tip: With three kids, I learned another great way to establish urgency is to count backward when you are asking them to do something. I used to count forward ("OK, I need you all to go get your pajamas on and get ready for bed. One... two... three... four... five"), and nothing would happen. I was just giving them a counting lesson (next time you go out, watch parents who do the count-forward approach and how it never works). I changed it up and started counting backward ("OK, I need you all to go get your pajamas on and get ready for bed. Five… four… three… two… one"). They never wanted it to get to one. There was running, hustling, and pajamas being flung everywhere. Count down for more urgency.

Establish Worst-Case Scenarios. While best-case scenario can be motivating, what truly motivates at home is the avoidance of pain. Clearly establish worst-case scenarios to incent action. To build on our example above, you can add onto your deadline for your children's room to be clean by stating your punishment if it is not accomplished. Example: "If I come in here at noon on Saturday and your room has not been cleaned, I will take all forms of technology from your possession for the next week." The same is true for your spouse and as stated above, it needs to be delivered a bit more measured. For example, "It is really important to me that you get X accomplished by Y date. I want you to understand how important that is to me. If you do not get it done as you have promised, not only will I have to find a way to get it done, I will likely be so upset with you, that I really don't know what I will do."

Sometimes the unknown is even scarier than the known.

Be Careful How Much You Use. Using too much urgency at home can be just as damaging as using too much urgency at work. One negative outcome is that your children and spouse stop listening to you. They experience you as *predictably dramatic*. Like the "little boy who cried wolf" fable, they don't know what is urgent and what isn't. They become numb to the heat.

I have recently learned that my three kiddos (Abby, seventeen; Noah, fourteen; and Aaron, twelve) have many inside jokes that all refer to my most monumental parenting fails. While the list is probably worthy of a book all on its own, one example pertains to this point. If any of my kiddos were here, they would tell you that I don't hold other drivers in particularly high regard. Let me explain. My general attitude is that if you see someone else driving a car, assume they are only halfway paying attention to what is going on around them. Between people's personal lives, work stress, and phones, the odds that someone is distracted is particularly high.

I *turn the heat up* on this message when it pertains to parking lots. In addition to the adage of "always look both ways," I have always stressed that you want to make eye contact with a driver if you are going to step out in front of their car, even if you have the right of way. (On a related note, next time you are driving in a grocery store parking lot, notice how few people actually do this and instead just step right out in front of your car. They have put their lives in your hands without even realizing it. Not me, brother.)

After my kids failed to get the point of my lesson repeatedly, I changed my language. I would point to a car and say to them, "See that car cruising through the parking lot? See how the driver is leaning over to grab something from the passenger seat while still driving? That car *would end you!*" My intention was that this message of imminent death (worse-case scenario) would yield a more serious response to my request. Logical, right? But parenting isn't logical. Instead, my kids now use that phrase with each other as a funny inside joke.

Noah: "Hey Aaron, you know what's going to happen if you don't get your homework done, right?"

Aaron: "No, what could possibly happen? It's not that big of a deal."

Noah: "The teacher might end you."

And if you are curious, my kiddos still walk out in front of cars without looking to this day. Too much "parenting hot sauce" not only loses the point, but it will serve as eternal comic relief.

The other outcome is potentially worse. Your children develop an internal anxiety that they carry with them throughout life. They become *hard-wired* to be anxious all the time. It burns them up from the inside out. Focused urgency is always the key.

Just as we can learn to master urgency at work, we can just as easily learn to master urgency at home. This not only allows us to regain control of our hectic lives, but it models for others a path of focus and intentionality. We don't have to be at the mercy of the endless plates of peppers being thrust in front of us each day.

CHAPTER 8 QUESTIONS TO CONSIDER

1. What are the "life peppers" that create urgency in your life?

    Where do you feel as though you are behind and/or aren't doing enough?

2. Make a list of all the items that are truly important and put them in the 90 percent circle. Now put everything else in the remaining 10 percent circle.

    *   Reflect on your circles. Notice the items in your 10 percent circle that you have given more time than you should. What has that cost you?

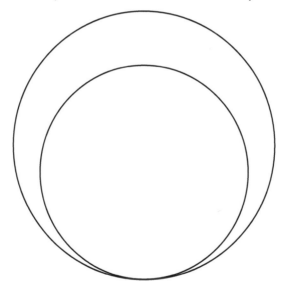

    *   For the items in your 10 percent circle, consider any of the following strategies to keep them in check:

— Offer fixed amounts of time to these activities (e.g., I can only give you one hour per week)

— Delegate

— Outsource

— Say "No"

3. What are the areas in your life that do require greater urgency?

How can you apply the principles of urgency toward those?

— CHAPTER 9 —
Mastering Urgency

 Several weeks after her instrumental meeting with Martin, Kate looked down at her phone. It was her boss, Martin. It was Monday morning at 5:30 a.m. and Kate was just leaving her workout class. She noticed that Martin was requesting an *emergency* meeting at 9 a.m. Kate could feel her anxiety rise ever-so-slightly. She quickly caught herself.

He's just anxious again about the status of our implementation, she thought to herself. *It is nothing that a quick phone call can't fix. Not to mention, I have my team meeting at that time, and I don't want to cancel it.*

Kate declined Martin's meeting invitation and texted him that she would call him on her commute into work.

When Kate got home from her workout class, the house was still. Neither of the kids had gotten up yet and Kate's husband, Mike, was just beginning to stir. Kate got in the shower and began reflecting on the calendar invite from Martin. Her thoughts naturally drifted to how much she and her team had gotten accomplished over the last few weeks. It had been challenging at work, to be sure, but there was a sense that her team was going to make it happen. Kate couldn't do much to control the load being placed on Martin. She knew he was under tremendous pressure from the rest of the senior leadership team to transform the organization's technology infrastructure as quickly as possible.

Yet, Kate also knew that this type of transformation required focus and precision from her entire team. It was no place for distractions or unnecessary and unwarranted pressure from overly anxious leaders. And Kate's team appreciated her approach. Kate protected the team's Monday morning meetings and never canceled them, regardless of the pressure that she might be feeling. Her team rewarded her steadiness and composure with a renewed sense of loyalty and commitment. Kate's team had been with her since her beginning of the company. While other parts of the company had seen continued turnover from key talent, Kate was an anomaly. Hands down, all of Kate's team members felt the changes that she'd made to how she was leading them were working. They were accomplishing more under her leadership over the last few weeks than any other time in their careers, and yet, they were feeling less burned-out than before.

Admittedly, the last few weeks at work hadn't been completely smooth. Kate's new role as air traffic controller was a tougher job than she had expected. Her team had done as they were instructed and directed all requests her way. On more than one occasion, she had had a very animated leader sitting (or in some cases, standing) in her office trying to convince Kate that her team needed to make their need a top priority. Kate felt proud that she'd been able to defend her team's time, explaining to other department managers that if their project didn't fit into her team and the company's key strategic priorities, it had to wait.

When the other managers had issues with Kate's response, she directed them to Martin. Thankfully, Martin had done his part as well. In the rare case that a leader had elevated their request to him, he always backed Kate. Martin understood what she was trying to do and could immediately see the difference in outcomes. Her team was moving the fastest of any team in his function, and he had no intention to do anything that might slow them down.

Kate did have one other trick up her sleeve. When the team got together to discuss the priorities that she and Martin had identified, she shared with the team her concern about other items being added to the *urgency* list, resulting in everything feeling urgent. To counter this, Kate had pulled out of her briefcase a brown paper bag. Kate reached into the bag and, one by one, pulled out three bottles of hot sauce that she'd discovered while searching for a treat for Ainsley.

She explained to the team that each bottle of hot sauce represented urgency. Rather than run the risk of everything eventually being covered in hot sauce, the bottles were there to make sure only a handful of initiatives could be urgent at any given time. If an initiative or project was deemed urgent by her, she would give a bottle of hot sauce to the owner of that respective project. The owner had to keep the hot sauce bottle until the project was completed. When it was done, the project leader would then return the bottle to Kate. She could only give out the three bottles, thus keeping herself and the team in check. Kate was particularly fond of how well this trick had seemed to be working thus far.

As Kate rinsed her hair, she shifted her thoughts to this past weekend. Her top performer, Amanda, had been gone the whole weekend with her husband for a well-needed and well-earned mini vacation. After Martin had his *talk* with Carlos discussing the real limitations that the organization was facing, he was successful in convincing Carlos to remove the hiring freeze and allow departments to staff up to meet the high expectations. In addition, he was also successful in getting Carlos to agree to provide raises and bonuses for critical team members.

As a result, Kate was able to win Amanda back before she started her new job. She knew how much effort Amanda had put in at the company over the last year. But, more importantly, she also knew how much Amanda and her family had sacrificed. It was Kate's recommendation that Amanda and her husband take the weekend away to reconnect. Kate had even helped find them someone to watch their kids while they were away.

Kate's weekend wasn't all that bad either. Her son had a baseball game on Saturday morning, and genuinely seemed to be enjoying himself, a big change from the season before. The parents and the coaches on that team seemed to be taking youth baseball way too seriously. Kate and her husband had time to go for a run together both Saturday and Sunday. It was their time to talk and reconnect. They had both decided that they were not going to push their kids to a level of overachievement this year. This particularly applied to their daughter. As a ninth-grader, Ainsley was already feeling an incredible amount of, frankly, unhealthy pressure from teachers, parents and other students to overachieve. Kate and Mike knew that there would be plenty of time for work and pressure in Ainsley's life. They wanted her to have the space to try new things and fail without fear of possible consequences.

All that said, Kate and Mike had to take away Ainsley's phone over the weekend because she'd failed to do her chores, including walking the dog, which had resulted in more than one mess that had to be cleaned up. It was a tricky balance. They wanted Ainsley to feel grounded, supported, and comfortable, but not too comfortable. She was a teenager, after all.

Every once and a while, she needed a fire lit under her to get her properly moving.

Kate noticed a large soap bubble on the glass of the shower. In that moment, it hit her. At work and in life, there was pressure coming from all directions, all the time. There was never enough time to get everything done that others expect. Not to mention, others' expectations are rarely realistic. Kate realized if she wasn't careful, everyone she was responsible for would be torn apart by all the demands. To protect herself and those in her care, Kate knew she needed to put a bubble around them. The bubble would cancel out the noise and allow her people to focus on what matters and what is truly important, without being confused by the constant urgency that tried to press in.

The bubble Kate was watching popped. *How fitting,* Kate thought. There will always be change and pressure to keep up with. That was life. That said, she knew how she chose to deal with that pressure was up to her. She would just need to make another *anti-urgency* bubble. And another.

Acknowledgments

This book has been an amazing and long journey. And as with any journey, there have been many companions along the way that offered me a word of encouragement, a valuable critique, a vote of confidence, companionship, and most importantly, the gift of their most precious resource: their time.

To my editorial board, enough thank yous will never fully honor the time, advice, and counsel that you provided. Cathy Fyock, Emily Smith, Randy Hain, John Kim, Wendy Case, and Kristen Leigh, you all gave time, attention, care, and perspectives that not only forced me to re-examine the book but also forced me to re-examine my voice. As a result, this book became a better book and I became a better author.

To Cathy Fyock, book coach extraordinaire, the book wouldn't have happened if you had not provided me the guidance, structure, and accountability that I so desperately needed. In a world filled with urgency, you helped me make this book a priority in a way that I couldn't on my own. Thank you for that tremendous gift.

To Henry DeVries and the team at Indie Books International, thank you for your guidance, prompting, cajoling, and encouragement to help me take this project over the finish line. Your work took a manuscript and made it into something I, and others, can touch and hold. For that, I will be eternally grateful.

To all my clients, thank you for sharing with me the intimate details of your lives. Without that gift, I would never be able to not only see the need for this book but also tell the real stories that are woven through this book. I hope that your stories of struggle and inspiration can be a gift to all of those who read this book.

To my amazing wife, Emily. Thank you for not only encouraging me but rolling up your sleeves and unleashing your tremendous gifts as a writer to help me shape this book into what it ultimately is. My journey with you inspired so many of the stories woven through this book.

And to Abby, Noah, and Aaron, thank you for being my spark of *urgency* to seek to push myself further and take on new and scary challenges. You three do it with the best of them and inspire me each day.

And to you, dear reader, thank you for investing your time with this book. I hope that it not only proved entertaining, but also gave you *hope and handles* as you seek to make your life and the lives around you better.

After all, that's what it is all about.

About The Author

Brandon Smith is a leading expert in leadership communication and curer of workplace dysfunction. Known as "The Workplace Therapist" and host of *The Brandon Smith* podcast, Brandon is a sought-after executive coach, TEDx speaker, and award-winning instructor. He is the founder of The Worksmiths, LLC, an executive coaching and leadership development firm whose clients include numerous Fortune 500 companies. Brandon has personally coached more than 1,000 leaders and executives across the globe representing both for-profit and not-for-profit organizations.

In addition, Brandon is a highly requested keynote presenter and leadership educator. Brandon has delivered keynote presentations and leadership development sessions to over 100,000 participants over the last decade. As an adjunct faculty member at multiple prestigious business schools, he has won over a dozen teaching awards for his work in the classroom. Brandon has been interviewed by NPR, Fox News, *The Wall Street Journal*, NBC, *New York Post, Fast Company*, CNN, and many other media outlets for his expertise in leadership and workplace dynamics.

Brandon received an undergraduate degree from Vanderbilt University with a concentration in communications and team dynamics. His graduate work includes an MS in counseling from Georgia State University as well as an MBA from Emory University's Goizueta Business School.

He resides in Atlanta with his wife, their three children, and two loveable pups.

For information on executive coaching, leadership development, speaking, and other services, please contact Brandon at:

email: **brandon@theworksmiths.com**

Website: **www.theworksmiths.com**

For additional resources by Brandon Smith on combatting workplace dysfunction:

Website: **www.theworkplacetherapist.com**

Podcast: **"The Workplace Therapist Show" – available on iTunes and Stitcher**

Or: **https://theworkplacetherapist.com/the-brandon-smith-show/**

Connect with Brandon on Social Media:

 Buff.Ly/253vokr

 Facebook.com/brandonsmithwpt

 Twitter.com/thewptherapist

 Instagram.com/thewptherapist

 LinkedIn.com/in/brandonsmithtwpt